THE EARLY CHURCH

FROM IGNATIUS TO AUGUSTINE

THE EARLY CHURCH

FROM IGNATIUS TO AUGUSTINE

BY

GEORGE HODGES

YESTERDAY'S CLASSICS

CHAPEL HILL, NORTH CAROLINA

This edition, first published in 2007 by Yesterday's Classics, an imprint of Yesterday's Classics, LLC, is an unabridged republication of the work originally published by Houghton Mifflin Company in 1915. For a complete listing of the books published by Yesterday's Classics, visit www.yesterdaysclassics.com. Yesterday's Classics is the publishing arm of the Baldwin Online Children's Literature Project which presents the complete text of dozens of classic books for children at www.mainlesson.com.

ISBN-10: 1-59915-196-0

ISBN-13: 978-1-59915-196-0

Yesterday's Classics, LLC
PO Box 3418
Chapel Hill, NC 27515

Preface

These chapters began as Lowell Lectures in 1908. The lectures were given without manuscript, and have been repeated in that form in Cambridge, in Salem, in Springfield, in Providence, Rhode Island, and in Brooklyn, New York. The first, second, third, and fourth were then written out and read at the Berkeley Divinity School, Middletown, Connecticut, as the Mary H. Page Lectures for 1914. In like manner the sixth, seventh, eighth, and ninth were given at Kenyon College, Gambier, Ohio, as the Bedell Lectures for 1913. The tenth was given in 1913, at Ann Arbor, Michigan, on the Baldwin Foundation. Finally, the lectures, as they now appear, were repeated in 1914 at West Newport, California, at the Summer School conducted by the Commission on Christian Education of the Diocese of Los Angeles.

The following extracts from a communication in 1880 to the Trustees of Kenyon College indicate the intentions of Bishop and Mrs. Bedell, founders of the Bedell Lectureship:—

We have consecrated and set apart for the service of God the sum of five thousand dollars, to be devoted to the establishment of a lecture or lectures in the Institutions at Gambier on the Evidences of Natural and Revealed Religion, or the Relations of Science and Religion.

The lecture or lectures shall be delivered biennally on Founders' Day (if such a day shall be established) or other appropriate time. During our lifetime, or the lifetime of either of us, the nomination of the lectureship shall rest with us.

The interest for two years on the fund, less the sum necessary to pay for the publication, shall be paid to the lecturer.

We express our preference that the lecture or lectures shall be delivered in the Church of the Holy Spirit, if such building be in existence; and shall be delivered in the presence of all the members of the Institutions under the authority of the Board. We ask that the day on which the lecture, or the first of each series of lectures, shall be delivered shall be a holiday.

We wish that the nomination to this Lectureship shall be restricted by no other consideration than the ability of the appointee to discharge the duty to the highest glory of God in the completest presentation of the subject.

The original sources from which a knowledge of this period is derived are readily accessible in translation. In *The Ante-Nicene Fathers* (8 vols.) the reader will find most of the writings of the Early Church under the Pagan Empire, to the year 325. *A Select Library of the Nicene and Post-Nicene Fathers*, in two Series (each of 14 vols.), contains the most important works of Christian writers from 325 till the beginning of the Middle Ages. The *first series* is given to Augustine and Chrysostom. The *second series* contains the books of the leaders of Christian thought and life from Athanasius to Gregory the Great. The *Church History* of Eusebius, extending to 324, has been translated and edited by Dr. A. C. McGiffert. The continuations of this history by

Socrates (324-439), by Sozomon (324-425), and by Rufinus (324-395) are translated into English,— Socrates and Sozomon in the *Second Series* of the *Nicene and Post-Nicene Fathers*. Dr. Joseph Cullen Ayer's *Source Book* for Ancient Church History contains significant extracts from the writers of this period, with interpretive comments. The first volume of the *Cambridge Medieval History* deals with the fifth century. Professor Gwatkin's *Early Church History to 313* and Monsignor Duchesne's *Early History of the Church* are recent aids to an understanding of these times.

My friend and colleague, Professor Henry Bradford Washburn, has read these chapters in proof, and I am indebted to him for many helpful suggestions.

GEORGE HODGES

EPISCOPAL THEOLOGICAL SCHOOL

CAMBRIDGE, MASSACHUSETTS

CONTENTS

CHAPTER I

THE ROMAN WORLD

I

The Lay of the Land

The Roman world was bounded on the west by the Atlantic Ocean, on the north by the Rhine and the Danube, on the east by the Euphrates, on the south by the Desert of Sahara. The Egyptian world had been dependent on the Nile; the Assyrian and Chaldean world had been dependent on the Tigris and the Euphrates; the Roman world enclosed the Mediterranean Sea.

Outside of these boundaries lay the greater part of Africa, of Asia, and of Europe.

In Africa were savage people, whose descendants even to this day are separated from civilization by the wide barrier of the desert.

In Asia were three nations whose history antedated the time when Athens and Rome were country villages. With China and India, the Roman world was connected by an adventurous commerce. Every year

1

merchantmen sailed down the Arabian Gulf and across the Indian Ocean to Ceylon. There they met traders from the ancient markets of the East, and returned with cargoes such as laded the ships of Solomon,— "ivory and apes and peacocks," with spices, gems, and rich embroideries. But Persia was an enemy. Beyond the Euphrates the Persians remembered the day when they had ruled the world, and prayed for another Cyrus who should make them masters of the world again. They menaced Rome continually. Sometimes they succeeded in destroying Roman armies. Once they took a Roman emperor captive, and the rumor drifted back to Italy that the King of Persia, whenever he mounted his horse, stepped on the emperor's neck.

In Europe, on the wide plains of Russia, in the thick woods of Germany, hordes of barbarians, impelled by mysterious forces such as summon the tides and the birds, were threatening the South. Already, in the Old Testament, the Book of Zephaniah was filled with the terror of the Scythians; and in the New Testament, the Epistle to the Galatians was written to the people of a province which had been seized and settled by invading Gauls. The Rhine and the Danube, rising only thirty miles apart, made a boundary line between the empire and these tribes, guarded by the camps of the legions.

Between Italy and Greece, the deep cleft of the Adriatic Sea divided the Roman world into two parts. The divided parts differed in tradition and in language. In the East—in Greece and Syria and Egypt—the Romans had conquered countries which had ancient and splendid traditions, and were more civilized than

2

their conquerors. In the West—in Italy and Spain and Gaul—the Romans had overcome peoples few of whom had any history, and who had imitated the civilization and adopted the traditions of their masters. As for language, Greek was spoken by all persons of education in the Roman world during the first and second centuries of our era. Marcus Aurelius wrote his "Meditations" in Greek. It was not until the beginning of the fifth century—almost at the end of the period which comes within the compass of our present study—that the West had a satisfactory Latin Bible. Nevertheless, as time passed, the Latin language spread though the Greeks despised it; and by and by in the West Greek was forgotten. Thus the conditions were prepared for the political and theological misunderstandings which eventually divided the West and the East.

The Roman world was filled with cities. The civilization was intentionally urban. The government encouraged the centralization of social life, gathering the people into municipalities, dignifying the great towns with stately public buildings, and providing places of amusement. Out of these central cities, men went to work on the farms, coming back at night. The ruins which are found to-day in places now desolate and remote show both the extent and the splendor of this civic life. Every city had its wall and gates. Colonnaded streets led to the forum. There was a public bath, and a public library, club-houses and temples, a theatre for plays, an amphitheatre for games. Water was brought in aqueducts from the neighboring hills for use in private houses, and for fountains in the squares.

In the multitude of cities, certain of them shone like the greater stars: in Italy, Rome and Milan and Ravenna; in Africa, Carthage and Alexandria; in Syria, Antioch and Cæsarea; in Asia Minor, Nicomedia and Ephesus; in Greece, the cities of the Pauline Epistles—Philippi and Thessalonica, Athens and Corinth; Constantinople appeared at the beginning of the fourth century.

The cities were connected by substantial roads. They penetrated everywhere, like our railways: for the sake of trade and of travel, for purposes of peace and of war. Straight they ran, across the valleys and over the hills, and were constructed with such skill and made of materials so lasting that many of them are used as highways to this day. From the golden milestone in the Roman forum they extended over the empire—to Hadrian's wall in Britain, to the oasis of Damascus, to the Cataracts of the Nile.

It was an age of travelling. The journeys of St. Paul, from Jerusalem to Damascus, from Damascus to Antioch, from Antioch to Cyprus and Galatia, to Athens and Corinth, to Malta and Rome, illustrate the facility with which men went from place to place. Along the roads journeyed government officials with numerous retinues, rich patricians going from their houses in the city to their houses in the country, leisurely persons out to see the sights, philosophical lecturers seeking audiences, Roman soldiers, Jewish merchants, missionaries of Isis and of Mithra, preachers of Christianity. Some walked; some rode on mules, which millionaires shod with silver shoes; some were borne in carriages made comfortable for sleeping or reading. Posts marked the miles. Every five miles there was a posting-station, with relays of horses in the stables, for hire. The messenger who carried the news of the death of Nero from Rome to Spain travelled at the rate of ten miles an hour. The aged bishop of Antioch, in a tragic emergency, went to Constantinople, eight hundred miles, in a week, over fresh-fallen snow.

The bales of the merchants contained linen from Egypt, rugs from Babylonia and Persia, silks from China, furs from Scythia, amber from the Baltic, arras cloth from Gaul, spices from Ceylon. The postmen carried letters, newspapers *(acta diurna)*, and books in handsome bindings or in paper covers from the publishers in Rome to the booksellers and the librarians in the provinces. It was an age of constant correspondence. Officials, all over the empire, made their regular reports to Rome. Much of our knowledge of the time comes from letters—epistles of Paul, epistles of Ignatius, epistles of Pliny, familiar letters of Ambrose to his sister. The last of the great Romans, Symmachus, kinsman of Ambrose, patron of Augustine, wrote nine hundred and fifty extant letters, occupying a disappointing amount of space in them with explanations why he had not written before.

The constant transportation and communication over these roads aided the extension of a new religion. So did the spread of commerce which established Jews in all important cities. So did the universal language which enabled the preacher to address the people directly, without the need of an interpreter. So did the imperial discipline, which made the roads of the Roman world more safe for unarmed travellers than roads in England in the eighteenth century. There was a cosmopolitan quality in the common life which did not appear again, after the fourth century, until it was restored by the railway and the telegraph in our own time.

II

The Emperors

The administration of the Roman world was centred in the emperor. He determined the general situation. If he was strong, the common life was up-lifted. If he was weak, selfish and pleasure-loving, he gave over the empire to his favorites, and the court was in confusion. He was an absolute monarch.

There were, indeed, certain restraints upon this imperial power. Nominally, the Senate must be consulted. But during the period with which we are now concerned, the Senate was in subjection. Practically, during a great part of this time, the army made the emperors. The Roman world, in this aspect of it, was a rough, military democracy. Emperors were chosen by the acclamation of the legions; at first, at the capital, where the soldiers put down one and set up another in return for competing imperial promises; then on the frontiers, exalting their own commanders, and sometimes choosing men who had risen to command from the lowest ranks.

Maximin the Goth was born a peasant. He was remarkable among his rude companions for his height and his strength: he was eight feet high, and could outwrestle anybody in the neighborhood. Thus he got into the army. He attracted the attention of an emperor by running for miles beside his horse over a rough country, and then throwing a dozen stout men in succession. He rose to be a captain, then a commander. He was made emperor by his troops. He never saw Rome; his court was in his camp.

Philip the Arabian, who succeeded him, began life as a brigand. He became a soldier, and his fighting qualities made him an emperor.

A world in which a Gothic peasant and an Arabian brigand could ascend the imperial throne had in its order an element of informality and of popular opportunity which may fairly be called democratic.

But, once upon the throne, the Roman emperor held possession of his high place, even above the law. Constantine could kill his wife and son, Theodosius could order the massacre of seven thousand citizens, Commodus and Caracalla could hunt their enemies through the streets of Rome like wolves in the woods. The emperor was independent even of public opinion. He feared only the soldiers and the assassins.

The period of the Early Church, after the Apostolic Age, from the days of Ignatius to the days of Augustine, begins about the year 100, by which time most of the books of the New Testament had been written, and ends soon after the year 400, when the barbarians were actively engaged in the destruction of the Roman Empire. It is divided into two parts at the year 313, when the Edict of Milan granted liberty in religion. Before that time the Roman court was pagan; after that time, it was nominally Christian.

The two centuries which thus make the first part of the history of the Early Church saw three eras of imperial administration.

For eighty years (98–180) there were four strong and good emperors. They were among the best of all the rulers of mankind. Under Trajan, Hadrian, Antoninus Pius and Marcus Aurelius the world was governed by philosophers, whose sincere intention was to rule their people well.

Then for eighty years (from the accession of Commodus in 180 to the death of Gallienus in 268) there were nearly twenty emperors, good and bad, but more bad than good. Thus the peace and prosperity of the second century were followed by the adversities of the third. Some of these adversities proceeded directly from the weakness or the wickedness of the emperors. Some were due to calamities of nature, to a singular series of storms, earthquakes, fires, floods, plagues, famines, like the outpouring of the vials of doom in the Book of the Revelation. Some accompanied the victorious inroads of national enemies from the north and from the east.

After that, for forty years (268–313) four strong emperors redeemed the situation and saved the state.

Claudius and Aurelian were victorious in battle. Probus reigned in such a time of peace that he employed his soldiers in the work of draining marshes. Diocletian in his court at Nicomedia eclipsed the splendor of Oriental monarchs. His abdication was followed by some confusion, out of which Constantine emerged triumphant.

The century which followed, being the second part of the era of the Early Church, was troubled by contentions between rival emperors, by wars of theology waged by Christians against Christians, and by the steady advance of the barbarians. In the history of this period (from the Edict of Milan in 313 to the death of St. Augustine in 430) there are four outstanding imperial names. Constantine (311–337) tried to make the empire Christian; Julian (361–363) tried to make the empire pagan again; Valens (364–378) tried to make the empire Arian. They were theological emperors. Theodosius (379–395) was the last ruler of the united Roman world. After him, the division between the East and the West became definite and permanent. He was followed by his incompetent sons, Honorius and Arcadius. Rome was taken by the Goths, and Carthage by the Vandals.

III

Society

The society of the Roman world in the age which thus extends from Trajan to Theodosius was composed, as we say, of higher and middle and lower classes. The higher classes were the patricians; the middle classes, the plebeians; the lower classes, the slaves.

The patricians were persons of ancient descent and abundant means. They held, for the most part, the great honorary offices, consular and senatorial. They lived in magnificent houses on the Palatine Hill, whose ruins still attest the spacious and luxurious manners of the time. In the summer, they retired to their villas in the country, among the mountains, by the lakes, and on the cool borders of the sea. They are described from the point of view of an unsympathetic outsider in the satires of Juvenal.

Juvenal had no part in the festivities of patrician society. He observed them from a distance, and in the spirit of the reporter who gets his information from the servants and writes it down for a constituency which is willing to believe anything bad about the rich. There were foolish and extravagant and vicious persons in that society, no doubt, as there are to-day under like conditions. But the great part of it was composed, then as now, of pleasant, kindly people, sometimes too content with their privileges and unmindful of the wants of their neighbors but living in dignity and virtue, and even in simplicity. There were extravagant and spectacular dinner parties; there were Roman ladies who eloped with gladiators. But these things are easier to write about than the plain goodness of decent domestic life, and have, for that reason, a prominence in the record which is out of all proportion to their importance.

We have an example of the high-minded patrician in Pliny. His people had lived by the lake of Como since the beginning of the empire. He had been brought up by an eminent soldier, who had been governor of Upper Germany, and had twice refused the acclamation of the legions calling him to the imperial power. He had had the advantage of the society of his uncle, Pliny the Elder, who was forever in pursuit of knowledge. From him he learned habits of literary industry, and of restrained and simple living. He was educated in Rome under Quintilian, who put the chief emphasis of his instruction on the moral side of life. There he came to know and revere the Stoics, the Puritans of their time, and to appreciate their severe virtues without following their skeptical philosophy. He served in the army as tribute of a legion. Then he entered upon the study of law, and attained conspicuous success in that profession. He had such charm of speech that a crowded courtroom attended upon his orations even when he spoke for seven uninterrupted hours. In the intervals of his legal business, he devoted himself to literature, read the classics and wrote books, which, according to the fashion of the time, he read aloud, as he did his speeches, to his friends. He wrote letters, which were afterwards published. One of them we shall find interesting and valuable in connection with the history of the Christians. He was made governor of the province of Bithynia, to straighten out its tangled finances. He lived happily with his wife, Calpurnia. When he made his long speeches she had relays of messengers to tell her how the argument proceeded from point to point. When she was absent he was not content unless he had two letters from her every day. In the summer, they went to one of their places in the cool country, delighting in the scenery, and in the progress of the farm. In his native place by Como, he paid a third of the expense of a high school, and endowed a public library.

These benefactions were characteristic of the time. Partly by tradition, partly by the urging of public opinion, the patricians exercised a splendid generosity. The Roman millionaire spent a great part of his money for the welfare and the glory of the city. The extant inscriptions record his gifts, endlessly. Now he built an aqueduct, now an arch; here he endowed a temple, there a public bath; sometimes he paved a road, sometimes he provided a feast for all the citizens, or a free show of gladiatorial fighting. Herod Atticus, who died in the same year with Marcus Aurelius, was the most liberal benefactor of the Roman world. To Olympus he gave an aqueduct, to Delphi a hippodrome, to Corinth a marble theatre roofed with carved cedar, to Thermopylæ a bath with a colonnade. Money, he said, is to be used for the common good. Gold which is not well spent is dead.

The plebeians included all of the free population under the patrician class. They were of all degrees of wealth and poverty.

Many of the wealthier of them had come into the Roman world as slaves, taken in war. But the wars of Rome were often fought with nations who were superior to the Romans except upon the field of battle. The slaves brought back from such wars were more intelligent, much more cultivated and in the higher arts of life more able, than their masters. The Romans put them in charge of their estates and of their business. The emperor found among them the most efficient public servants, whom he might place over the departments of state. Under these conditions many slaves purchased their liberty. They applied themselves to trade, to commerce by land and by sea, to the management of factories and mills. Some of them grew very rich. Some of them were sore beset by the temptations which lie in wait for those who have suddenly exchanged poverty for wealth, being millionaires who had no traditions and did not know what to do with their money.

Over against the picture of the patrician Pliny we may set the picture of the plebeian Trimalchio, to whose famous banquet we are bidden in Petronius's novel, the "Satiricon." Trimalchio had been brought as a slave from Asia, in his childhood. He had won the affection of his master and mistress, and had inherited their property. So extensive were his investments in exports and imports that a single storm on the Mediterranean had cost him a million dollars. In his gorgeous house were four vast banqueting halls. His bees came from Hymettus, his mushroom spawn from India. He owned estates which he had never seen. Now he gives a dinner. One course represents the signs of the Zodiac. Then follows a boar, served whole, with baskets of sweetmeats hanging from his tusks; in rushes a huntsman and stabs the boar, and out fly thrushes which are caught in nets as they fly about the room. Then the ceiling opens, and down comes a great tray filled with fruits and sweets. The meal is accompanied by singing and instrumental music, and floods of wine. Trimalchio is a man of letters, and a poem of his own composition is recited, in which famous heroes and heroines play strange parts. Niobe is imprisoned in the Trojan horse, Iphigenia becomes the wife of Achilles. Rope dancers amuse the company. Gradually, wine overcomes the hosts and guests. Slaves come in and take their places at the table, while the cook gives an imitation of a favorite actor. Trimalchio and his wife have a lively quarrel, in the course of which he flings a dish at her head. Finally, the noise is so great the town watch come running in thinking that the house must be on fire.

The rich plebeians are better represented by the fine tombs which they built for themselves and their families, whereon they caused to be inscribed, like armorial bearings, the symbols of their honest trades.

But most of the plebeians were poor. They were impoverished in part by the extension of patrician estates which drove men from the farms, and in part by the presence of a vast population of slaves by whom most of the work of the community was done. Even for such poor folk as these, however,—the tenement lodgers of our modern cities,—there were pleasures in the civic life. The public baths were municipal club-houses. There were marble benches by the playing fountains along the shady streets. There were numberless fraternities, some of them organized on the basis of social congeniality, some on the basis of a common trade, to which a poor man, even a slave, might be admitted. There were public dinners, on festal occasions, served on tables spread in the streets for all the people. The women had their societies. The mothers' clubs determined the fashions and the social behavior of Rome.

Among the public pleasures a great place was held by the plays and the games. The theatre, which among the Greeks had given opportunity to the highest genius of the race, was mostly abandoned by the Romans to triviality and indecency. The plays were of the order of low-class vaudeville. The greatest interest centered in the amphitheatre. When Vespasian built the Colosseum he made forty-five thousand seats, and there was standing room for five thousand more. The area could be planted with trees for forest-fights with wild beasts, or flooded with water for battles of boats. There the tragedies were actual tragedies. The spectacle was so fascinating that Tertullian, in order to keep the Christians from attending it, promised them far more delightful spectacles in heaven where they should look down upon the agonies of persecuting princes and hostile heathen roasting in the flames of hell. And Augustine tells of a friend who being urged to go to the games against his will resolutely shut his eyes. Instinctively opening them at the sound of a great cry, he could not get them shut again.

Below the plebeians were the slaves. They made a great part of the population. A large house might have four hundred of them, a large estate four thousand. By some they were regarded as humble friends; some doubted whether they had human souls. They were in some measure protected by the law, but well into this period of history a lady might have her slave whipped to death if she broke a mirror; and at best

15

they were in the bonds of servitude, with all which that inevitably implies on both sides, for the slaves and for their masters.

IV

Religion

The Roman world, thus constituted politically and socially, was filled with interest in religion. There had been a time of scepticism, when the sacred institutions of Numa had been discredited and neglected. The philosophers had resolved the gods into ancient heroes magnified, or into personifications of the powers of nature. The temples had been deserted and the venerable liturgies forgotten. But this was only one of the ebb-tides in the ever-moving sea of human life. The years of spiritual dearth were followed by years of spiritual plenty. The first three centuries of the Christian era were marked by a general enthusiasm of religion. Christianity began in the midst of a religious revival.

One of the manifestations of this religious spirit was a widespread interest in Greek philosophy.

The Epicureans, indeed, denied the essential propositions of religion—the providence of God and the immortality of the soul. The gods, they said, dwell serenely aloof from human life, having no interest in our concerns; and the soul is perishable.

But the Stoics vindicated the everlasting reality of religion. They believed in a living God, immanent in the world. All things are therefore good, and the wise man will so regard them, no matter how bad they seem to be. "Everything," says Marcus Aurelius, "is harmonious with me which is harmonious to thee, O universe. Nothing for me is too early or too late, which is in due time for thee." All men are brethren, having one divine father. The artificial distinctions which divide society, even the differences which appear in nations and in races, have no real existence. We are all members of one body. It is the divine intention that we shall love one another. The highest good in human life is to live virtuously and to serve our neighbor. Stoic teachers were going about making converts to these excellent doctrines, preaching sermons, comforting the sad, directing the perplexed, and giving counsel to disturbed consciences.

Plutarch, who rejected the philosophy of the Epicureans because of their materialism, and the philosophy of the Stoics because of their pantheism, believed in the personality of God, following the revived philosophy of Pythagoras. The Pythagoreans realized the difference between good and evil, attributing evil not to God but to matter. Thus they distinguished between the spirit and the flesh in man, holding that the spirit is in bondage to the flesh and can attain its freedom only by abstinence and purification and the subduing of the senses. They had their saints, by whose example they were inspired. While the Christians were reading the lives of Christ, the pagans were reading the lives of Pythagoras and of Apollonius of Tyana. They found a place for all the ancient gods, who entered their monotheistic system as angels and archangels.

Another manifestation of the contemporary religious interest was the welcome which was given in the Roman world to religions from the East.

From Phrygia came the religion of Cybele, the Magna Mater, the Mother of the Gods. Her Asiatic priests came with her, bringing their strange language and strange ceremonies, worshipping a meteoric stone. With Cybele came Attis, a god who being violently put to death had come to life again. On the 24th of March, called Sanguis, the day of blood, the votaries of this religion mourned the death of Attis, as the Hebrew women in the vision of Ezekiel had mourned the death of Tammuz. They lamented with wild cries, and horns and drums and flutes, with mad dances. On the 25th of March, called Hilaria, they celebrated the resurrection of Attis, with rejoicings equally unrestrained, with feasts and masquerades and revelry.

From Egypt came the religion of Isis and Osiris (= Serapis). After a baptismal initiation, the disciple passed through successive grades of approach to a central secret which was disclosed to those only who had thus made themselves ready to receive it. Daily services of litanies and hymns, matins and vespers, following immemorial usage, attended the opening and the closing of the shrine. On the 28th of October was enacted in a kind of passion play the death of Osiris, killed by Set the god of evil, with weeping and mourning. Three days after, the lamentation was changed to cries of joy: "We have found him, let us rejoice to-gether!" Osiris had risen from the dead.

These religions, together with that of Mithra, which we will consider later, were mystery religions. They led their disciples on from grade to grade till they were taught at last a doctrine too sacred to be told to the common world. This doctrine, connected with the nature myth of the dying and reviving god, was a doctrine of redemption. It was at the heart of these religions as it was also at the heart of the Orphic mysteries of Dionysus, and of the Eleusinian mysteries of Demeter. Attis, Osiris, Dionysus, Demeter,—each is a god who dies, and rises from the dead. Each is a symbol of the great course of nature wherein vegetation dies from off the face of the earth in the winter and appears again alive in the spring. Each represents a primitive belief that man must somehow enact this necessary order, by his mourning and rejoicing, in order to make sure that, after the winter, spring will follow. Each religion lifted this physical idea to a spiritual significance, and from the miracle of the resurrection of the plants inferred the miracle of the resurrection of the body, and the immortality of the soul. These were, accordingly, redemption religions, helping men out of the slavery of sin, and promising them life everlasting.

But the philosophers—Epicurean, Stoic, Pythagorean—and the priests, with their mysteries from Phrygia and Egypt, touched only a few of the people. In the main the Roman world continued in the old religion.

The old religion was indeed attacked by the influences of foreign conquest. The victors brought back in triumph to Rome not only the kings of vanquished peoples but their gods. It was discovered that they were many in number, with perplexing similarities and dissimilarities. Also the old religion was attacked by the invasion of knowledge. The boundaries of the region of mystery in which the gods dwelt were set back. The world was better understood. It was perceived that some of the events of life could be explained by other reasons than those which were pronounced by priests.

It was perceived, also, that whole tracts of life were beyond the range of the conventional religion, which took no account of sin and made no provision for salvation. The old religion was prosaic and practical. The purpose of it was to secure the favor or avert the anger of the gods, and this was done by mercantile transactions—so much paid and so much obtained in return. Spiritual needs were not considered, spiritual blessings were not asked nor desired. The contention between light and darkness, between summer and winter, between life and death, which in the East symbolized the contention between good and evil in the soul of man, was indeed represented in the mythology of Greece and Rome, but it was only faintly reflected in religious aspiration. When the sense of sin and the consciousness of the necessity of salvation awoke in the Western mind they found no satisfaction in the official religion.

Nevertheless, the ancient ways remained. The creeds and rites of the old time continued to be observed by ignorant persons, by peasants on farms and in villages, and by those who were naturally conservative, to whom any change from the traditional order involved the probability of some sort of bad luck. They continued to be observed also by cultivated persons, by whom they were associated with art and letters, with the refinements of society, and with the long past. Among these people the ceremonies of religion were family customs, connected with distinguished and revered ancestors. In spite of all the criticisms of sceptics, and the discontent of devout souls, the old religion dominated the Roman world. Christianity found it everywhere in control. Everywhere it pervaded the whole of life.

It was a domestic religion, associated with every detail in the conduct of the household. The door was consecrated to Janus, and the hearth to Vesta. The house was under the protection of the Lares, the contents of it were guarded by the Penates. Ceres presided over the growth of the grain; Flora attended to the blossoms, and Pomona to the fruit in the orchard. There was a divinity for every act of life from birth to death. And neglect of the invocation of the proper god at the proper time was likely to involve serious consequences. There is an ancient instinct, which we formally discredit and call superstition, which whispers to the soul of man that he would better do what his fathers did before him. It is one of the silent forces which they who were converted out of paganism had to defy. When things actually did go wrong, in those days when the relation of effect to cause was very imperfectly perceived, even the Christian was tempted to think that the old gods were taking their revenge.

The Roman religion pervaded all the affairs of business. Not only were the transactions of exchange and barter, the occupations of industry, and the administration of law, conducted in the language of religion, under the patronage of the gods, but it touched all manner of employment. With its shrines and temples and images and liturgies, it engaged the services of the mason, the carpenter, the blacksmith, the goldsmith, the weaver, the dyer, the embroiderer, the musician, the sculptor and the painter. The schoolmaster gave instruction in its sacred books. Sowing and reaping depended on it. War waited for it. In a time when fighting was considered a normal part of the life of man, and the army was the most important institution of the state, the site of every camp was marked by the shrines of the soldiers, and the captains consulted the will of heaven before going into battle. When they were victorious, they all joined in a public thanksgiving to the gods. Religion entered into every department of civil life. Nobody in the employ of the government could possibly evade it. Every office had its sacred image. Every oath was taken in the name of the gods. Every senator as he entered the Senate-house cast grains of incense into the fire which smouldered before the statue of Victory.

The ancient religion included in its province all kinds of social pleasure. Its well-filled calendar abounded in festivals, which called the people together for processions and sacred feasts, with lighting of lanterns and decoration of house-doors with wreaths. To it were consecrated the theatre and the amphitheatre, and the plays and games were offered to the gods, like the sacrifices on the altars, as a vital part of religion; the idea being that the gods were as much interested in athletic sports as men.

To break with the Roman religion was thus to sever one's self from almost the entire round of social life. Even in the epistles of St. Paul we see what possible compromises might be involved in accepting an invitation to dinner, the meat of which might have been offered to an idol. What could a Christian do in those cities where there was an image of a god at every corner of the street, and where the entrance into every shop and market, into every employment, industrial, civil or military, and into every kind of amusement, was through some sort of pagan rite! The Christians stood apart from the common life. They were considered by their perplexed neighbors to be enemies of society.

And this religion was not only thus inclusive and pervasive, but it was of obligation. The emperor was the official head of it, and was himself divine among the gods. The political value of such a doctrine is evident enough, and it did not seriously offend men in those days when even the greatest of the gods were hardly more than human beings magnified, and when a god could be welcomed into Rome, or else expelled, by an act of the Senate. The emperor was the embodiment of the empire. The worship of the emperor, which consisted in burning incense before his statue, was a declaration of allegiance. Among the many and various religions, East and West, over all the local and provincial cults, this was the one universal creed. Otherwise, one might select and reject; Rome was tolerant of all religious differences; the only limit to religious liberty was the law which forbade men, in the zeal of their own creed, to deride or assault their differing neighbors. But the emperor must be worshipped by every man: that was imperative. To refuse this worship exposed the Christian to the charge of conspiracy or treachery against the state.

It was in the midst of such a world—political, social and religious—that Christianity appeared, a strange, unparalleled and menacing phenomenon. The world received it with instinctive enmity. The new religion was compelled to struggle for its life.

CHAPTER II

THE STRUGGLE FOR LIFE

At home, among their kinsfolk and acquaintance, the Christians were met with immediate hostility. They were put out of the synagogues, and worse punishments were visited upon them.

In the Roman world, they were at first treated with contempt and aversion, and then persecuted. The persecution increased from attacks on individuals and groups to concerted municipal and even imperial action against Christian society. Twice the government made an organized attempt to destroy the obnoxious religion.

I

The Tolerant State Persecutes the Benevolent Church

That Christianity should have been thus received in the Roman world is remarkable, because one of the most notable characteristics of the church was its benevolence, and one of the most marked characteristics of the empire was its tolerance.

The church was a benevolent institution. There is indeed a benevolence which seeks mainly to improve the intellectual, moral and spiritual condition of the neighborhood. It endeavors to impose its own interests and enthusiasms upon those who are interested in other aspects of life. It has new standards, and calls for conformity to them. It says, You must be like us. And this is instinctively resented by the neighbors, who hate to be reformed. But the benevolence of the church appeared in the effort to mitigate conditions which all men desire to have changed. The Christians ministered to the sick and to the poor.

The church remembered the social precepts and example of Jesus Christ. His constant emphasis on the supreme value of brotherly love—extended not only to the least human creatures but even to the most hostile—set the note of the ideal life.

Thus the first recorded act of the Christian ministry was the healing of the sick, when Peter and John made a lame man to walk, at the Beautiful Gate of the Temple. Thereafter, the Christians did that kind of helpful service every day. It was confessed by their neighbors, even in the midst of the accusations which pronounced the Christians the most unsocial people of all people, that they were very kind to all who were in trouble. It was perceived that when the plague came the Christians stayed and nursed the sick, while others fled; and it was seen that this fraternal care was bestowed not only on the brethren in the society, but on all who needed it, without distinction.

The first recorded act of the Christian congregation was the appointment of persons to attend to the feeding of poor widows in Jerusalem. Thereafter the records of Christian ministration to destitute, overlooked and unprotected persons continued without interruption. The first account of a Christian service, after the New Testament, is Justin Martyr's description of a friendly feast, sacramental but social, at which a collection was made for the assistance of the poor. The church was the association wherein the rich and the poor met together, and at first, as in Jerusalem, had all things in common. St. Paul was engaged on his missionary journeys not only in the preaching of sermons and the founding of churches, but in gathering Gentile money for the support of poor Christians in Jerusalem.

Not only was the church devoted to the practice of benevolence, but the state was committed to the principle of tolerance. The pagan state was tolerant of religious differences to an extent to which the Christian state, when its turn came, showed no parallel until very recent times. It is true that in the reign of Tiberius votaries of Isis were expelled from Rome; but that was on account of scandal. It is true that the Jews were similarly treated in the time of Claudius; but that was on account of a riot. And these expelled persons, after a decent interval, quietly returned. Eclecticism, as a free choice among the gods; syncretism, as a combination of creeds; mysticism, as a subordinating of all forms of ritual and religion in the endeavor to find God in direct communion with the unseen, were characteristic of the age. It was permitted to men of letters to ridicule or deny the gods. Courteous consideration was given even to so exclusive a religion as that of the Jews. No people were persecuted for their religion, except the Christians.

The tolerant state persecuted the benevolent church for two reasons: first on account of a general dislike, then on account of an increasing dread.

Dislike of the Christians colors the earliest references to them in contemporary writing. It appears in Tacitus, in his history, where he speaks of the Roman Christians in the reign of Nero (A.D. 64). It appears also in Pliny, in his letter concerning the Christians of Bithynia in the reign of Trajan (113).

In the history of Tacitus, the Christians are disliked on the ground that they are enemies of society.

The rumor spread in Rome that the great fire which destroyed a considerable part of that city had been set by Nero. He was notoriously fond of fires, and had been heard to say that if the world should ever burn, as some predicted, he hoped that he might live to see it. And he was the only person whom the conflagration benefited. It cleared the ground for extensive building operations which he had long desired to undertake. At last, when the common talk began to take on an ugly tone, so that Nero feared a mob, it seemed wise to divert the blame. It was laid upon the Christians.

The Christians were exposed to such a charge because they were "queer." They were unlike their neighbors. Thus they encountered that tremendous social force which makes for uniformity. Society, by a kind of instinct, resents the assertion of difference. Even to-day, when it is more hospitable to dissent than it has ever been since the foundation of the world, it still insists on observance of the common customs. Any nonconformist, in dress or in behavior, is immediately ridiculed. Formerly such a person was stoned, or hanged, according to the degree of his offence. The Christians were queer. They stood apart from both the religion and the recreation of their neighbors: they hated the images which all other people worshipped, and the games which all other people enjoyed.

The Christians were not only queer but mysterious. They met in private houses, secretly, under cover of night. Nobody knew how many they were, and ignorance magnified their number into portentous proportions. Nobody knew what they did when they met together. Thus they were easily accused of abominable practices. Vague rumors, beginning with mistaken reports of Christian sacraments, declared that they put infants to death, and that they ate human flesh. Even in our own time the idea of ritual murder makes its way easily from one to another in Russia, and is believed by persons who are otherwise intelligent.

Therefore Nero put the blame upon the Christians. Many were arrested, and on confession that they were Christians were condemned. Some were sent into the arena to be torn by wild beasts; some were smeared with pitch and made to serve as flaming torches along the paths of the imperial gardens. This, we are told, continued until Rome was weary of it. In a city accustomed to the tragedies of the games, where sympathy was dulled by the daily spectacle of pain, this implies some extended space of time.

The charge of incendiarism fell to the ground, but the dislike continued and increased. Tacitus says that the Christians were enemies of civilization, being filled with hatred of society *(odium humani generis)*. From that time, Christianity was a capital offense. There seems to have been no law to that effect, but a precedent was established. The cases of the Christians came up not in the civil courts but in the police courts, and were disposed of by discretion rather than by legislation. From the year 64 a Christian was exposed to arrest and capital punishment, like a brigand or a pirate.

In the letters of Pliny, the Christians appear as persons obstructive to business.

A manuscript came to light in Paris, about A.D. 1500, which contained the correspondence between Pliny and Trajan. It was seen and used by a number of persons during several years, when it suddenly disappeared and has never since been found. There is no question as to its authenticity, but its appearance and disappearance, like the passing light of a comet, show how little we know about the conditions of life among the Christians in the beginning of the second century. For only in the pages of this fleeting manuscript have we any information concerning the distresses of the Christians in Bithynia. It is an easy inference that there were a hundred similar persecutions about which no record or tradition has remained. Even in the New

Testament there are intervals of silence, so that no-body knows, for example, what St. Paul did for ten years after his conversion. It is as if we were reading a history in which pages have been torn out by the hand-ful. There was a persecution under the emperor Domi-tian, about 95, which the author of the Epistle to the Hebrews may have been expecting when he cited, for the inspiration of those who had not yet resisted unto blood, the examples of the heroes and martyrs of old time; it may have been the distress referred to in the First Epistle of Peter, where some suffered not as a thief or a murderer, but "as a Christian."

Pliny was sent out as governor to Bithynia and parts adjacent. The province lay east of what we now call Constantinople, and north of the Syria, Cilicia and Cappadocia of the Acts of the Apostles. It formed the southern shore of the Black Sea. There had been much mismanagement of governmental affairs there, especially in finance, and Pliny was appointed to bring the confusion into order. In going about the country on this errand, he came upon the Christians.

He found so many of them, both in villages and cities, that in some places the temples were deserted. He proceeded against them on the basis of informa-tion brought to him, and according to the custom which had prevailed since the days of Nero. But the matter was complicated by two considerations: in part by the fact that great numbers of persons were thus incriminated, especially on charges made by anony-mous letters; and in part by the fact that some who were accused confessed that they had once been Chris-tians,—some said twenty-five years ago,—but had long since repented of that error. How ought such cases to be treated? And, even where the case was plain, what ought to be done with such a multitude of offenders?

Pliny wrote to Trajan for instructions. Shall I punish the Christians without regard to age or social situation? Shall I pardon those who are willing to renounce Christianity? Shall I proceed against the Christians as Christians, or only by reason of offences? Pliny told Trajan what he had learned from peasants, and from such of the faithful as he had examined under torture. They are harmless people, he said, who meet daily to sing hymns to Christ as to a god, to partake of a common meal of innocent food, and to bind themselves to do no wrong. He remarked incidentally that dealers in fodder for animals to be used in sacrifice had begun to return to their business.

Trajan replied that obstinate adherence to the Christian name must be punished as usual, but that nobody is to be sought out, or arrested on any anonymous accusations. The penitent, he added, may be pardoned.

Pliny's remark about the fodder suggests the second cause of the general dislike. In the time of Nero, the Christians were disliked for social reasons. They interfered with business. The fodder-sellers of Bithynia objected to them, like the image-makers of Ephesus. Behind the persecution of the Christians in the Roman Empire there were economical causes,— trade antagonism.

To the dislike with which the Christians were regarded in the Roman world was added, as a second reason for their persecution, an increasing dread. They were feared by the two extremes of society,—by the poorest and most ignorant of the people on the one side, and by the best and wisest on the other. They were hated alike by the masses and by the magistrates.

The dread of the Christians by the masses was based largely on superstitions. The people were in fear of the gods. When calamity came—plague, earthquake, fire, flood, defeat in battle—they saw in it the anger of the gods. This was the universal doctrine of the ancient world. The second century was a time of unusual disaster, and the third was little better. There were portents in the earth and in the sky and in the sun. There was distress of nations with perplexity, such as seemed to indicate that end of all things which was predicted in the Gospels. To the general mind it was plain that there was indignation in heaven. The gods were sore displeased.

It was also plain that the Christians were the enemies of the gods. All other men accepted the current theology. The philosophers, indeed, conformed without much faith; some of them ridiculed the gods. And the Jews conformed from motives of prudence, denying the existence of all gods but their own, but not making a serious protest. The only non-conformists were the Christians; and theirs was an aggressive and militant non-conformity. They were not content to absent themselves from the temples and to abstain quietly from recognition of the divinities of Rome. They vigorously spoke against them. They boldly denounced idolatry, and destroyed idols. They were accounted atheists and antagonists of the gods.

The logic of the situation was plain. When any community was visited with calamity—if fire broke out, if plague appeared—the blame fell on the Christians. They had provoked it. The gods had sent it because of Christian impiety and insult. Let the Christians, then, suffer for their sins. Let the angry gods be pacified by Christian blood. "The Christians to the lions!"

Even the magistrates shared in the dread thus arising from superstition, but they had also a more serious reason for alarm in the political situation. They saw the essential need of unity. The empire was composed of conquered provinces, held together by force of arms. The state lived in continual peril of revolution. The least appearance of disaffection must be met with immediate restraint by the local magistrate. Even the assembling of small companies of men in associations professedly social but possibly disloyal was forbidden by the government. Pliny asked Trajan to permit the organization of a fire company at Nicomedia, but Trajan refused. He was willing to provide improved apparatus, but he would not let the men hold meetings. The incident shows the nervousness of the administration.

The empire was in peril not only from revolt but from invasion. Along the frontiers were powerful enemies, civilized and uncivilized, waiting on any appearance of weakness to break the barrier. The situation demanded unfailing loyalty. Any civil strife might bring the empire to destruction.

Thus we may understand the possibility of such a tragedy as the massacre of the Theban Legion. In the latter part of the third century (268) there was a peasant's war in Gaul. The peasants arose against the landlords and burned their houses. Thus they protested against the situation which had become intolerable. The emperor Maximian, whom Diocletian had made his colleague in the West, marched with an army to put the peasants down. Before the battle, the emperor summoned the army to pray for victory; that is, he directed the observance of certain rites appealing to the Roman gods. The Theban Legion, which was composed of Christians, refused to take part in these prayers. The emperor directed that the legion should be decimated. But the killing of a tenth of the men did not dismay the others, and again the legion was decimated, and so on till it was destroyed. The story may not be true, but it illustrates the state of mind of Roman generals who found soldiers in the ranks whose Christian consciences forbade them to obey orders.

Thus it was that the tolerant state persecuted the benevolent church. The Christians were disliked, for reasons partly social and partly commercial; and they were dreaded as being hostile both to the gods and to the empire. And they were continually increasing. Nobody knew where the evil might next appear, perhaps in his own family. Christianity seemed like a contagious disease, like a plague whose nature was not understood and for which there was no remedy, in the face of whose silent and secret progress men grew desperate.

Moreover, the Christians invited intolerance by their own intolerant position. The religious liberty of the empire had only two limitations. It was required that everybody should leave his neighbor's religion alone; it was also required that everybody should pay to the official religion—especially as represented by the image of the emperor—the decent respect of outward conformity. The Christians defied these limitations. They declared, both in season and out of season, that all religions but their own were false; and they refused to render even the outward form or reverence for the emperor's image as a symbol of the state. Publicly and persistently they invited enmity, as the outspoken enemies of all the religions of their neighbors.

II

Local Persecutions

The age of persecution includes first a period of local attack. Now in one place and now in another, arising for the most part from the dislike and dread of the masses of the people. A public calamity was likely to be visited upon the Christians. Then follows a period of general attack, in the time of Decius and Valerian (in the middle of the third century), and in the time of Diocletian and Galerius (in the beginning of the fourth). On each of these occasions the Christians were under the ban of imperial decrees by which the government was endeavoring to destroy them. The purpose was to maintain the unity of the empire.

An adequate history of the age of persecution will never be written. It is as impossible as to write an adequate history of the distress and tragedy of any war. Certain general facts may be set down, certain figures may be added up: so many martyred here and there and in such and such inhuman ways,—so many slain with the sword, so many burned with fire, so many stoned to death, so many frozen with cold, so many starved with hunger, so many drowned in the sea, so many scourged with whips, so many stabbed with forks of iron, so many fastened to the cross. Even on the statistical side the record is incomplete. But if we were to multiply the figures by two or by five, still we should be dealing only with the pains of body. We should miss the vital facts of faith and courage and self-sacrifice and glad devotion which made the martyrdom significant.

Out of the general terror, however, there are stories which illuminate the darkness. Sometimes when the martyr was a person of more than usual importance, or the torture was more fierce, or the courage was more fine than usual, some who stood by wrote a record, and the narrative, passed from hand to hand and read in secret meetings of the Christians, remains for us to read to-day.

Ignatius was bishop of Antioch at the beginning of the second century, while Pliny was in Bithynia. Under circumstances of which we are not informed, he was arrested and condemned, and sent to be put to death in Rome. He seems not to have possessed the privilege of Roman citizenship, else he might have been exempt from that form of punishment. A sentence in one of his letters suggests that he may even have been a slave before he became a bishop. Such a social position would have been in accord with the conditions under which the church was then recruited, and would have expressed its splendid disregard of the artificial positions of society. The bishop was to be exposed to wild beasts in the games of the Colosseum. He was put in charge of a company of ten soldiers, who, he says, made the whole journey a long martyr-dom. Thus they traversed the country by the road which ran from Antioch to Troas, across the length of Asia Minor; thence to Philippi, and so by land and sea to Rome.

It was a very humble and pathetic triumphant procession. In every town the Christians met the mar-tyr and ministered to him, and from neighboring places, off the line of the journey, the churches sent delegations of devout people with messages of faith and sympathy. In two cities, on the coast of Asia Minor towards Europe—in Smyrna and in Troas—he stayed long enough to write letters. In Smyrna, he wrote to those of the churches whose messengers had met him—the Ephesians, the Trallians, the Mag-nesians—and a fourth letter to the church of the city which was his journey's end,—the Romans. In Troas, he wrote three letters, two to churches which he had visited, in Philadelphia and Smyrna, and one to the bishop of Smyrna, named Polycarp. Other letters were added to this list by the zeal or error of a later time, but these seven are authentic.

The letters show a keen sense of the perils of division. It was reported to Ignatius, as it had already been reported to St. Paul from Corinth, that there was disagreement among the Christians. Even in the face of persecution, when all their strength was needed against a common enemy, they were contending among themselves. This was due in part to the novelty of the situation. The new churches were formulating their faith and organizing their life by the process of experiment. Such a process involved discussion, and discussion disclosed the inevitable differences which belong to human nature. Some men were conservative, some were progressive. A new sense of freedom increased the eagerness of these debates.

Against the individualism thus appearing, Ignatius protested. In the strongest language he urged the people to stand together, to subordinate their differences, and to be loyal to their bishops. "Obedience to the bishop," he said, "is obedience to God." "We ought to regard the bishop as the Lord himself." "Do nothing apart from the bishop." "He who does anything apart from the bishop serves the devil." These vigorous sentences provided material in later years for the use of churchmen in controversy with their brethren who were in a state of schism. But the intention of Ignatius was practical rather than ecclesiastical. The bishop as the pastor of the church was the appointed leader of the congregation. He was the natural centre of the unity of the people. Their progress, even their existence, depended on the strength of the united brotherhood.

The chief interest of the martyr, however, was in his approaching martyrdom. He wrote to the Romans begging that they would not intercede for him, nor try to save him. "Grant me nothing more than that I may be poured out a libation to God." "Come fire," he cried, "and iron, and grapplings with wild beasts, cutting and manglings, wrenching of bones, breaking of limbs, crushing of the whole body; come cruel tortures of the devil to assail me! Only be it mine to attain unto Jesus Christ." "I write you in the midst of life, eagerly longing for death."

With these seven letters, thus illuminating for a moment the way on which he went rejoicing to his death, the saint goes forward on his journey and is seen no more. Polycarp sent copies of some of them, perhaps of all, to the Christians of Philippi, at their request. Thus they were preserved. Then on some Roman holiday, in the crowded Colosseum, Ignatius was devoured by beasts.

Polycarp, the bishop of Smyrna to whom Ignatius wrote, was born about A.D. 69, the year before the destruction of Jerusalem. He spent his youth in Ephesus, the city which for a time after the fall of Jerusalem became the centre of Christian life and activity. Tradition finds St. Philip near by, in Hierapolis, and locates the closing years of St. John in Ephesus itself. Polycarp would have been about thirty years old when St. John died.

To Polycarp, Ignatius wrote with affection, giving him encouragement and counsel, as an elder brother to a younger. "Be diligent," he said, "be diligent. Be sober as God's athlete. Stand like a beaten anvil."

Among the disciples of Polycarp at Smyrna were two young men, Irenæus and Florinus. Florinus afterwards fell into heresy and Irenæus, who had by that time become bishop of Lyons, wrote to dissuade him. In the course of his admonitions he reminded Florinus of their old teacher. "I can tell," he said, "the very place in which the blessed Polycarp used to sit when he discoursed, and his manner of life, and his personal appearance, and the discourses which he held before the people, and how he would describe his intercourse with John and the rest of those who had seen the Lord, and how he would relate their words. And whatsoever things he had heard from them about the Lord and about his miracles or about his teaching, Polycarp, as having received them from eyewitnesses of the life of the Word, would relate altogether in accordance with the Scriptures. . . . And I can testify in the sight of God that if that blessed and apostolic elder had heard anything of the kind, [i.e., such as Florinus was foolishly maintaining] he would have cried out, and stopped his ears, and would have said after his wont, 'O good God, for what times hast thou kept me, that I should endure these things,' and would have fled from the very place where he was sitting or standing when he heard such words."

Irenæus remembered also concerning Polycarp that one day meeting the heretic Marcion in the street in Rome, Marcion said, "Don't you recognize me, bishop?" and Polycarp replied, "Indeed I do. I know you very well; you are the first-born of Satan!"

These incidents attribute to the saint a narrow mind and a hasty temper, and disclose a disposition to meet error by the easy but entirely ineffective method of abusing the heretic rather than by the difficult but only convincing method of reasoning with him fairly. The impression which they make upon the modern mind is somewhat mitigated by the story of the dealings of Polycarp with Anicetus, bishop of Rome. The two bishops represented the two parts of the Roman world, Greek and Latin, East and West. They conferred as to the true date of Easter. According to the common usage of both East and West, the date of Easter was decided by the Jewish Passover, and the Passover was determined by the vernal equinox, and the equinox was the day of the month which the Jews called the fourteenth of Nisan, and the Christians called the twenty-first of March. The full moon after the equinox marked the day of the Passover. The Eastern Christians kept the Easter on the day, whether it was a Sunday or not; it might be a Monday or a Friday. The Western Christians waited for a Sunday. Polycarp informed Anicetus that the Eastern custom was authorized by the word of St. John himself. The apostolic precedent was entirely on his side. It is an interesting fact that this argument made no impression upon the mind of Anicetus. He liked the new way better; the argument from authority did not greatly appeal to him. The bishops, however, agreed to disagree. Neither could convince the other, but neither carried the disagreement to the extreme of excommunication. The bishop of Smyrna celebrated the holy communion at the altar of the bishop of Rome, and returned, leaving his blessing.

At last in Smyrna, at a festival season, the pro-consul—the Asiarc—being present and presiding at the games, a number of Christians were arrested, for some cause unknown, and were ordered to immediate execution. They were exposed to the lions, in the amphitheatre. A cry arose for Polycarp, and mounted police found him, in his country-place, and took him to the city. On the way the chief of police met him, the brother of an eminent and devout woman in the bishop's congregation. He took Polycarp into his chariot, and tried in a friendly way to persuade him to offer incense in order to conciliate the mob, but to no purpose. Then, losing his temper, he threw the old man out into the road. The stadium was crowded when the guards arrived with Polycarp, and a great roar of hostile shouting greeted him. But he heard a steady voice saying, "Polycarp, be strong and play the man." The proconsul urged him to give up his foolish faith and abandon his disciples. "Disown them," said the proconsul, "cry, 'Away with the atheists!' " And this the martyr did, facing the crowd, and crying, "Away with the atheists!" but it was plain that he and the proconsul meant quite different persons. "Come," said the judge, "revile Christ, and you shall go free." Polycarp answered in words which have never been forgotten. "Fourscore and six years have I served Him, and He hath done me no wrong. How then can I speak evil of my King who saved me?" Then in the arena they heaped wood together, and tied him to a stake, and burned him. And the faithful gathered his charred bones together, and laid them up as sacred treasures,—

Assured the fiery trial, fierce though fleet,
Would from this little heap of ashes lend
Wings to the conflagration of the world.

When Irenæus, the disciple of Polycarp, became bishop of Lyons, he took the place of Pothinus who with others of his flock had been put to death for loyalty to the name of Christ. In Pater's "Marius the Epicurean" (pp. 421-426) the hero of the book coming in the dark of the early morning to a celebration of the sacrament, hears a reading of the letter in which the survivors of the persecution in Lyons describe the tragedy to the churches.

The common hatred of the Christians had been increasing in Lyons, and they were insulted in the streets. A rumor, generally believed, accused them of abominable crimes, especially declaring that they followed the example of Œdipus, who had married his own mother, and of Thyestes, who had eaten his children. The conditions were such as have preceded, in our day, the massacre of Jews in Russia. Christians were hooted, stoned and beaten. Then, in the absence of the Roman governor, some were imprisoned until his return. He caused them to be examined with torture so cruel as to call out a public protest from one of the brethren, Vettius Epagathus, a man of distinction in the city, who asked to be permitted to testify that "there is among us nothing ungodly or impious." He was thereupon thrust into prison with the others. The examination of certain pagan slaves of Christian masters added to the popular fury, for they declared that all the accusations were founded upon fact.

The wrath of the people, and of the governor, fell with special force upon Sanctus, a deacon from the neighboring town of Vienne, and upon Blandina, a slave girl, weak in body but invincible in spirit. They were tortured until their continuance in life seemed miraculous. Finally Sanctus was roasted in the arena in an iron chair, and Blandina, thrown in a net before a wild bull, was gored and trampled to death. Attalus, having been led around the arena with the inscription, "This is Attalus the Christian," was burned in the chair; and Ponticus, a boy of fifteen years, died after "the entire round of torture." These all agreed in crying in the midst of their pain, "I am a Christian, and no evil is done amongst us." The bishop Pothinus, being ninety years of age, died in prison, after being beaten by a mob. The bodies of the martyrs were burned to ashes, and the ashes were swept into the Rhone.

A little later, in the beginning of the third century, occurred the martyrdom of Perpetua and Felicitas. This took place in Carthage, when Septimius Severus was emperor of Rome, and at a time when the birthday of his son Geta was being celebrated. The narrative appears, for the most part, in the words of Perpetua herself. She was a lady of good birth and education, twenty-two years old, married, and having an infant son. Felicitas was a slave girl. They were arrested, with other young people, while they were receiving Christian instruction, not yet having been baptized. Perpetua's father, a man of gray hairs, begged her day after day, for his sake, and for her child's sake, to deny the Christian name. And these importunities added to her distress. But she continued constant. One night, in the prison, she dreamed that she saw a golden ladder reaching up to heaven, having sharp weapons fastened to the sides, and underneath a great dragon, "who lay in wait for those who ascended, and frightened them from the ascent." Up this she climbed, setting her feet on the head of the dragon, and came into a garden where one in white, dressed as a shepherd, bade her welcome. Saturus, the teacher, was devoured in the arena by a leopard; Perpetua and Felicitas were tossed and gored in nets.

III

General Persecutions

If now we multiply these four stories indefinitely, to the fury of the masses add the deliberate policy of the magistrates, and extend the time over a space of ten years twice, we get an idea of the two general persecutions, the Decian and the Diocletian.

The Decian persecution began in the middle of the third century. The empire had been celebrating the thousandth anniversary of the founding of Rome (A.D. 248). It was an occasion which summoned all patriotic and reflective persons to compare the present with the past. The comparison gave no ground for satisfaction. Roman power was failing, Roman character was degenerating. To the fear of the Goths was added the fear of the Persians. The emperor Decius, coming to the throne in these evil times, felt that the first step toward a restoration of the Roman valor was a revival of the fine old Roman virtues, and it seemed to him that the best way to bring back the old victorious virtues was to restore the old religion. To this, accordingly, he addressed himself, and began his campaign for reform with a resolute attempt to destroy what he considered to be the chief obstacle in the way of his pious restoration. Following what seemed to him the commands of conscience, and acting in the sincere spirit of patriotism, honestly desiring to do what was best for the empire over which he ruled, he endeavored to eliminate the Christian Church.

The imperial decree called upon all persons to declare their loyalty to the Roman religion by offering sacrifice. After a long period of general peace, during which many had become Christians conventionally, without individual conviction, the decree was answered by the submission of multitudes. Some cast incense on the altar willingly; some came so pale and trembling that "the crowd mocked them as plain cowards who dared neither die nor sacrifice." Some purchased certificates to the effect that they had complied with the decree, though they had not, and the word *libellus*, certifying such a certificate, gave to these persons the name *libellatics*, by which they were unfavorably known after the persecution was over. Hardly, however, had these troubles fairly begun, when Decius went to fight the Goths, and was killed in battle.

Valerian, the successor of Decius, continued the persecution. A man of advanced years, and of blameless life, a friend of Christians, he saw the empire beset on every side by powerful enemies. He saw that the only safety lay in united strength. He had reason to suspect the loyalty of the Christians; at least, there were some among them who were eagerly anticipating the ruin of the empire. Commodian, in his "Carmen Apologeticum" was watching for the end of the world. "Soon the Goths will burst against the Danube, and with them comes Apollyon their king to put down by arms the persecution of the saints. Rome is captured. Goths and Christians are as brethren." Accordingly, the good Valerian carried on the contention which the good Decius had begun. To the demand that every Christian should renounce his religion by offering sacrifice, he added a prohibition of Christian meetings, even in the catacombs.

Then when Xystus, bishop of Rome, defied the decree by publicly transferring to the catacombs the bodies of St. Peter and St. Paul, the tragedy began. The bishop of Rome was martyred in the catacombs. Cyprian, bishop of Carthage, was beheaded. The sentence which was pronounced upon Cyprian expresses the mind of the persecution. "Your life, Cyprian, has long been a life of sacrilege; you have gathered around you many accomplices in your criminal designs; you have set yourself up as an enemy to the gods of Rome and to their sacred rites; nor have the pious and deeply revered emperors Valerian and Gallienus been able to bring you back to their religion. Therefore, as the upholder of a great crime, as the standard-bearer of the sect, I must now make an example of you in the presence of your associates in guilt. The laws must be sealed with your blood. Our sentence therefore is that Thascius Cyprianus be put to death with the sword."

That was in 258. Two years later, Valerian in defeat was captured by the Persians, and was never seen again. The persecution was thus concluded. It had, indeed, disclosed at the beginning a shameful number of Christians whose religion has no serious significance, but it had finally shown a strength in the church which the whole power of the state had not been able to subdue.

The Diocletian persecution fell upon the Christians in the beginning of the fourth century, after more than forty years of peace. During those years Christianity had been steadily growing; Christians had found their religion no hindrance in the way to high office in the state; many of them were in the palace. Splendid churches in all the greater cities bore witness not only to the popularity of the Christian religion, but to a general opinion that the days of persecution were ended finally.

The conditions which gave rise to renewed contention against the church do not appear plainly. No unusual disasters or defeats suggested that the Christians were again angering the gods. The opposition may have been steadily but quietly increasing in proportion to the success of Christianity. To the patriotic Romans who felt that the church was a serious menace both to the Roman religion and to the Roman character, every new ecclesiastical building was a reason for alarm. The matter would lie heavily upon the conscience of a good man like Diocletian. It is said that one of those who urged him to do something about it was his aged mother, a devout pagan.

Then, one day, the occasion of an imperial sacrifice, the gods gave no omen; heaven was silent. The officiating priest informed the emperor that certain Christians had been observed making the sign of the cross. It was their presence which had been resented by the gods. This incident precipitated the persecution. On the morning of the feast of the Terminalia, being the twenty-third of February, 303, the great church of Nicomedia, over against the emperor's palace, was torn down. An edict was published condemning all the Christian churches to a like demolition, and ordering the surrender and destruction of all the Christian books. The persecution was directed not so much against the Christians individually, as in the days of Decius, as against the Christian society, in its officers, its buildings, and its books. Even these milder measures were in many cases enforced with intentional carelessness on the part of officials who were indifferent or sympathetic. They were willing to accept any books which the clergy might surrender, without looking too curiously to see whether they were sacred books or not. The rigor of the persecution depended on the temper of the local ruler. In many places, there were hardships and tragedies. A mob officially incited to pull down a church will not spare the clergy or the congregation. The Christians themselves were not disposed to look with forbearance on their brethren who tried to escape the storm. The demand that the books be surrendered must not, they said, be evaded; it must be defied. There appeared a new kind of offender. To the *libellatic* of the Decian persecutions was now added the *traditor*, the man who gave up the books, the betrayer of his trust, the traitor.

Then Diocletian retired from the throne of the empire; Galerius, who succeeded to his power, and renewed the persecution, died of a loathsome disease; and new men with a new perception of the significance of Christianity, men like Constantius, and Constantine, his son, appeared upon the scene.

The Edict of Milan, set forth in the year 313 by Constantine and Licinius, gave to the Christians and all others "full permission to follow whatsoever worship any man had chosen." The places of Christian worship which had been taken away, whether by purchase from the state or by imperial gift, were to be restored. "Those who restore them without price shall receive a compensation from our benevolence." Thus it was hoped that "whatever divinity there is in heaven" would be benevolent and propitious to the imperial government, and to all under its authority. With this edict the age of the persecutions came to an end.

Not only had the persecutions failed to destroy the church, they had mightily assisted it. They had made the profession of Christianity a serious matter, involving great peril and demanding courage. They had exposed every believer to the danger of the loss of all of his possessions, even of life itself. They had excluded from membership in the church all merely conventional and half-hearted persons. And the courage of the martyrs had attracted into the church the bravest spirits of the time. They had exhibited the true credentials of Christianity. They had commended their religion by the witness of their endurance for the love of Christ. Men are asking, "What is this new religion?" and were being answered by the patience, the devotion, the splendid consecration of the noble army of martyrs.

CHAPTER III

THE DEFENCE OF THE FAITH

I

Against Prejudice

The first antagonist of the Christian faith was prejudice.

This was partly in consequence of the astonishing novelty of the Christian ideas and ways, and partly in consequence of the secrecy under the cover of which the Christian movement proceeded. The early service, which assembled the Christians before sunrise, was made necessary by the fact that every day was a working-day,—unless it was a pagan festival,—but still more by the need of seclusion from intruding enemies. It is easy to see how the enmity and the seclusion acted and reacted, one upon the other; how fear, on the one side, led the Christians to keep themselves apart from their neighbors; and how zeal, on the other side, inclined the honest, pious and scandalized neighbors to believe regarding the Christians, the current tales and rumors in which imagination supplied the lack of knowledge.

The Christians were accused of atheism, because they denied all the gods which other men revered, and had no images to represent any deity of their own. They were accused of sedition, because nobody knew what they might be planning in their secret meetings, in the dark. What did they mean by the social democracy which they called brotherhood in Christ? What was the general revolution for which they were waiting and praying, which was to begin with a destruction of all civilization in a conflagration of the world, and was to result in the kingdom of heaven? They were further accused of immorality, an accusation which they themselves afterwards brought into their own fraternal disputes as one of the counters of controversy, but to which color was given by the secrecy of their meetings and by misunderstanding of their sacrament.

This position of general prejudice against Christian religion was honestly held by excellent and intelligent persons. To Tacitus, for example, at the beginning of the second century, Christianity was beneath contempt; it was the degraded superstition of ignorant and vulgar people. To the judges who in the middle of the third century pronounced their sentence upon Cyprian, a Christian bishop was living a life of sacrilege, and was upholder of a great crime.

Marcus Aurelius, imperial philosopher and moralist, saw nothing in Christianity to attract him. In the single sentence of the "Meditations" in which he mentions the Christians he despises the obstinacy with which they maintain their opinions even to the pain of death. This was partly temperamental. Marcus Aurelius was a hesitant and indecisive person, a type of a perplexed generation, believing and disbelieving. He offered splendid sacrifices to the gods, whose existence he was inclined to doubt. He disliked the savage games in the Colosseum, which, nevertheless, he attended, taking with him, however, a book which he diligently read in the midst of the excitement of the audience. "Hope not," he said, "for Plato's Republic; but be content if the smallest thing advance,"—a wise counsel for a poor man tempted to dream what he would do if he were king, but a foolish counsel for a king to give to his own soul, who being king is bound not only to hope for Plato's Republic, or whatever better ideal commonwealth he knows about, but to strive to realize it in his own kingdom. This temperamental individualism of Marcus Aurelius kept him from understanding what seemed to him the obstinacy with which Christians gave their lives for the brotherhood, in the hope of the kingdom of heaven.

But the blindness of the emperor was shared by all the eminent men of the day. The most important movement in the history of man, which was speedily to take possession of the Roman Empire and to build a new Rome by the Bosphorus, and thereafter to determine the progress of civilization, and to save out of the wreck of barbarian overthrow the books of the very men who were writing at the moment in utter ignorance of the meaning of this struggling and despised religion—this movement began and continued with no attention from the wise and the great. They either overlooked it, or regarded the Christians as an insignificant Oriental sect.

Lucian, in the second century, mentioned the Christians in a satire. His favorite literary form was the dialogue. He wrote imaginary conversations, into which he introduced the heroes, the philosophers, even the gods. They talked very freely together, in the inspiration of the agreeable hospitality of Lucian, and one who is admitted into their informal society gets glimpses of the mind of the century. Lucian stands in no great awe of the gods. There are now so many of them, and from such strange lands, and with such extraordinary manners that Zeus, in one of the dialogues, proposes to appoint a membership committee of seven gods to pass on all new applicants for admission to Olympus. In another dialogue, old Charon comes up from the Styx to see why it is that so many of the passengers on his ferry-boat are sad and reluctant, and prefer life to death; he comes up to see what there is in life which makes it so attractive,—and returns more perplexed than before.

Proteus Peregrinus, a character in one of Lucian's dialogues, is a wandering impostor who pretends to be a Christian. He finds the Christians simple and credulous persons, who take him at his own valuation, making no inquiries. Being put in prison for the Christian name, he finds that they spare no pains to minister to him. From earliest dawn widows and little children are waiting for the opening of the prison doors to bring him food. Men of rank visit him, and read to him from their sacred scriptures. Even from neighboring towns people came to comfort him, and to labor for his release. "Why," says Lucian, "these poor wretches have persuaded themselves that they are going to be every whit immortal, and live forever; wherefore they both despise death and voluntarily devote themselves to it, most of them. Moreover, their first law-giver persuaded them that they are all brothers one of another, when once they come out and reject the gods of the Greeks and worship that crucified Sophist, and live according to his requirements."

Lucian was a mocking spirit, but Celsus was a serious philosopher, a conservative person, who resented the dissent of Christianity from the standing order. All that remains of the writings of Celsus is contained in quotations which Origen made for the purpose of refuting him. These fragments show that he was offended by the social position of the Christians. He disliked them for their poverty and ignorance. They seemed to him presumptuous and impertinent people who undertook to be teachers, having never learned. He was disgusted with their insistence upon confession of sin, and the pride which they seemed to him to take in having no health in them; they spoke like worms in the mud. He objected in much the same spirit to the doctrine of incarnation, which degraded the idea of God. He attacked the miraculous element in the Christian records, declaring it to be unhistorical and impossible. As a philosopher, intent on the pursuit of truth, he resented the doctrine of faith, which was offered, he thought, as an easy way to attain that which the student gains with labor and difficulty; it puts the ignorant on an equality with the educated; it leads only to illusion.

"Let no man come to us who is learned or wise or prudent; but whoso is stupid or ignorant or babyish, he may come with confidence. The only converts we care to have (or indeed can get) are the silly, the ignoble, and the senseless, the slaves, the women and the children." Thus Celsus, in the "True Word," expressed what he understood to be the position of the Christian Church. "Do not examine; only believe"; this, he said, was the Christian principle, to be abhorred of all philosophers.

Against the common prejudice and misunderstanding, a defence was made by the Apologists. Most of the early Christian writers were apologists, justifying the position of Christianity and attacking heathenism. That was their imperative business. Even at the end of the period of the Early Church, at the beginning of the fifth century, Augustine must devote half of his great work, the "City of God," to a refutation of pagan error. The name, however, applies more strictly to a few men who addressed their writings to the Roman emperors,—to Hadrian, to Antoninus Pius, to Marcus Aurelius. Chief among these was Justin Martyr.

Justin was born in Palestine, at Sychem, where Christ talked with the Samaritan woman by the well. His parents were pagans; his original and continuing interest was in philosophy. He desired to know the truth, and especially the truth concerning God, and the relation between God and the world. Thus he went, he says, to the Stoics, but found that they had nothing to tell him about God; then to the Peripatetics, who offended him by their anxiety regarding their fees; then to the Pythagoreans, who required him to pass an entrance examination in music, astronomy and geometry—how, they said, could he understand divine truth if he had not, by such studies weaned his soul from his senses? Finally, he found some satisfaction among the Platonists, who held out to him the hope of attaining to the sight of God.

But one day, as he wandered in meditation along the shore of the sea, he met an old man of venerable appearance who referred him to the apostles and prophets. These, he said, were not guessing at the truth, neither were they demonstrating divine things by reason, but were witnesses to the truth which they had themselves experienced. To them Justin went, and became a Christian. Thenceforth he devoted himself to the work of teaching what he had learned. He did not seek to be ordained, but as a layman, wearing his philosopher's cloak, he became a wandering lecturer, making his way from Ephesus to Rome, where he died by martyrdom.

Justin addressed two apologies—or, as we would say, defences of the faith—to Marcus Aurelius. They give us some idea of Christian life and faith in the middle of the second century.

There is not as yet any system of theology. There is no creed. The Christians are studying the New Testament, and drawing inferences from it, sometimes wisely, sometimes unwisely. Justin is a firm believer in the evidential value of Old Testament prophecy. He has much to say about devils, whom he is inclined to identify with the pagan gods. He expects a literal millennium. "I," he says, "and whoever are in all points right-minded Christians know that there will be a resurrection of the dead and a thousand years in Jerusalem, which will then be built, adorned, and enlarged as the prophets Ezekiel and Isaiah and the others declare."

There is not as yet any system of church government or worship. There are congregations whose chief officer is called the president, having deacons to assist him. There is an informal service of Bible-reading, preaching and praying, with a distribution of bread and wine. "On the day called Sunday, all who live in the cities or in the country gather together in one place, and the memoirs of the apostles, or the writings of the prophets, are read so long as time permits. Then when the reader has ceased, the president verbally instructs and exhorts to the imitation of these good things. Then we all rise and offer prayers. And, as we have said before, when we have finished the prayer, bread and wine and water are brought, and the president offers prayers and thanksgivings according to his ability, and the people assent, saying Amen. And then there is a distribution to each and a participation in the eucharistic elements, and portions are sent to those who are not present, by the deacons."

The emphasis of Justin is on the righteousness of the Christians, against the slanders of the pagans. The heart of Christianity is right conduct. Justin exemplifies in his own manner of writing that brotherly spirit which he says is characteristic of Christianity. He has no anathemas for his pagan neighbors. He believes that the divine influence of Jesus Christ touches all men everywhere; the Word is sown in all hearts; the Light lighteneth every man. All good living and good thinking are essentially Christian.

II

Against Heresy

The second antagonist of the Christian faith was heresy.

Heresy is partial truth. All profound truth, especially when it deals with that which is divine and eternal, has two sides. It has a nearer side which the mind may apprehend, and concerning which it is possible to make clear and definite statements. It has also a farther side, beyond all human apprehension, extending into infinity. The heretic is the man who, having attained certain definite ideas of truth, cries, "Now I know it all." Standing on the shore of the ocean, and looking out over the illimitable deep, he thinks he sees the other coast. He does see land, but the sight means that he is looking not over the ocean, but over some little bay or inlet of it. The heretic has a complete system of theology. This also is the refutation of heresy. There can be no complete solution of any equation which contains the factor of infinity.

The most eminent heretics of the second and third centuries were the Gnostics. The name signifies their claim of complete knowledge. Gnosticism arose from an honest desire to make Christianity a consistent intellectual system, to provide for it a theology which should appeal to men of learning and reflection. Such men were beginning to come into the church, bringing their intellectual habits with them. They were somewhat dismayed at the informality of the current Christian thinking, and undertook to introduce into it the element of order.

In the endeavor to state the Christian religion in such a way as to appeal to the cultivated mind, these men found two difficulties. There was a difficulty in the reconciling of the Old Testament with the New; partly in the matter of morals, where the New Testament was evidently on a higher plane; and partly in that contrast upon which St. Paul had insisted between the gospel and the law. There was also a difficulty in reconciling the condition of the world with the idea of God—the bad world with the good God; involving the everlasting problem of the origin and significance of evil.

Studying these difficulties in the light of contemporary philosophy, the Gnostics worked out certain cardinal positions. They maintained (1) that matter and spirit are essentially antagonistic, even as light and darkness, and as good and evil; matter being wholly evil. They held (2) that there are two worlds, a lower and a higher; a lower world in which spirit is imprisoned in matter and is striving to get free; and a higher world inhabited by divine beings, whom they called æons, emanations from God, some of them very near to God in His infinite distance, others nearer to the world. They said (3) that one of these æons, whom they named the Demiurge, made the lower world, and him they identified with the God of the Old Testament; and that another æon, whom they named the Christ, came to redeem men from the lower world, to liberate them from their bondage to matter into the freedom of the spirit. They taught (4) that the Old Testament, which describes the administration of the Demiurge may be treated with great freedom; there is no need to believe or to obey the teachings. As for the Christ, the supreme and saving æon, (5) He had no real body; the essential evil of matter made that impossible; the incarnation, the crucifixion, the resurrection, were only in appearance. They held (6) that Christ saves men not by any sacrificial atonement, but by illumination, by shining in their souls. This illumination shines effectively in the souls of the receptive, whom they called Gnostics, as possessing knowledge, while ordinary, dull and unreceptive Christians had nothing but faith. The Gnostics had immediate access to God, all other being distant from Him. They were in a Covenant of Works.

There were fanatical Gnostics, such as the Carpocratians, who finding the law to be the work of the Demiurge despised it, and disobeyed it on principle; or the Ophites, who, perceiving that the serpent in Eden was an enemy of the Demiurge, applauded the serpent and brought in serpent worship out of immoral pagan cults; or the Cainites, who for a similar reason canonized Cain and all the other Old Testament antagonists of God—the martyrs of the flood, the martyrs of the Tower of Babel, Saint Korah, Saint Dathan and Saint

Abiram. These men brought scandal upon the Christian name, and seemed to verify the worst rumors of pagan enmity.

But most of the Gnostics were honest and earnest men. They believed themselves to be upholding the spirit against the letter, the gospel against the law, spiritual religion against material religion. They felt they were fighting over again the splendid battles which St. Paul fought. Such Gnostics were Valentinus and Marcion.

Valentinus concerned himself with the problem of the relation between the good God and the bad world. This he solved by the doctrine of a series of æons; first a group of eight, the Ogdoad, beginning with the Unutterable and the Silent, from whom proceeded Mind, Truth, Word, Life, Man, Church; then a group of ten, the Decad; then the Dodecad. Wisdom, last-born of the Dodecad, aspired to know the Unutterable. In the midst of her vain struggles to attain this forbidden knowledge she gave birth to another æon, called the Desire of Wisdom, who was immediately expelled from Heaven. The Desire of Wisdom became the mother of the Demiurge who made the world. Some men he made spiritual, having in them a spark of the celestial fire which the Desire of Wisdom brought from above. Some men he made material. The material men are incapable of salvation; the spiritual men, called Gnostics, are certain of it. Between the two, the Demiurge made ordinary men, psychic men, who may be saved by help from on high. To save these men came new æons, Christ and the Spirit of Jesus. Men's salvation depends upon their receptivity to these divine influences, a receptivity which is assisted by the practice of asceticism.

This Valentinian scheme, fantastic in form, is in reality a statement of theology in terms, not of ideas but of persons. It is a kind of philosophical poetry.

Marcion concerned himself with the problem of the relation between the New Testament and the Old. In his sober and prosaic Gnosticism, the Valentinian angels and archangels had no place. Marcion applied to the current Christianity what he believed to be the principle of St. Paul. Finding Paul and the other apostles at variance, he threw out what the apostles, in error, had maintained; first, the whole Old Testament, as a book of the law which Paul had rejected; then those parts of the New Testament which seemed to him unpauline. He retained a single Gospel, mainly that of St. Luke, and ten of St. Paul's epistles, somewhat expurgated. Upholding, as he believed, a spiritual religion in opposition to religion debased and materialized, he held that the humanity of Christ was only in appearance. Christ could not have taken our material flesh, which is essentially evil. We ourselves, being unhappily combined with flesh, must release ourselves from it by ascetic practices.

Gnosticism, thus variously presented by Valentinus and by Marcion, offered to its Christian disciples a new statement of religious truth and a new kind of religious life. The Gnostics were gathered into fraternities, over against the orthodox. Not only the theology but the unity of the church was menaced. The agreement of the new teaching with the doctrines of the remoteness of God and of the evil of matter, which the West was eagerly receiving from the East, gave it popularity. It seemed to meet the objections brought by Lucian and by Celsus. Out of the common crowd of ignorant Christians it selected an exclusive company of cultivated persons who despised the flesh and devoted themselves to the study of philosophy. It claimed a superior knowledge, by virtue of which it interpreted the Christian religion to suit its own ideas.

A notable reply to Gnosticism was made by Irenæus. He wrote a book with the large title "Against Heresies." In it he described the opinions of Valentinus and Marcion and a host of lesser Gnostics, as if a plain description of their foolish notions must be of itself a sufficient refutation; and over against their errors he set the true doctrines of the Christian religion. It was impossible, however, to evade the fact that the Gnostics had raised a new question which demanded a reply. They had made it necessary for theologians to consider the test of truth. How shall we know the truth? The Gnostics claimed to be the only true teachers of Christianity. They claimed that their societies were the only true Christian churches. To the natural answer of the orthodox that the Scriptures were against them, they replied by a criticism of the accepted Scriptures which enabled them to reject whatever was out of accord with their beliefs.

Under these circumstances, Irenæus brought forward the argument from tradition. He said that the test of Christian truth is its agreement with the teachings of the Lord and His apostles, and that the question of such agreement is to be referred in every case to the churches to whom those teachings were committed. Such a reference made it necessary to identify the apostolic churches; especially, so far as possible, to name the men who in order, from the apostolic days, had held the episcopal office in them. Thus the rise of heresy and the endeavor to meet it by tradition set a new emphasis upon the organization of religion. It showed that the bishop was a person whose value was not only administrative but evidential; and that the evidential value of the bishop depended greatly upon the care with which his direct and orderly succession from the apostles was secured.

Irenæus said to the Gnostics, If you would know whether your teaching is Christian teaching or not, ask the nearest bishop, who received that teaching from his predecessor, and whose predecessor received it from the apostles. Such an argument came naturally from Irenæus who had himself been taught by Polycarp, who had been instructed by the apostle John.

The effect was to emphasize the idea of the church; and so much the more because Marcion's fraternities were claiming to be the true churches. The claim was refuted by the same reference to history. You are not true churches unless you can show that your ministers are successors of the apostles. Whatever looseness of organization had preceded the appearance of Gnosticism was now amended. It was necessary for the defence of the faith that the church as the guardian of the sacred tradition should be a definite society.

It was also necessary that the heretic, being thus referred to the church that he might compare his new doctrine with the old tradition, should find the tradition definite. There must be a creed. Potentially the creed, like the church, had existed from the beginning. Not only were the materials of it present in the Scriptures, but some brief formula had long been provided for use by those who came to be baptized. Little attention, however, had been given to the matter. The formulation of truth in a creed was as tentative and local as the organization of life in a church. The errors of the Gnostics hastened the making of a creed. Accordingly, in Irenæus and in other writers of the time, there appear endeavors to state in compact form the chief doctrines of Christianity. "The Church," says Irenæus, "though dispersed through all the world to the ends of the earth, has received from the apostles and their principles belief in one God and the Father Almighty, Maker of heaven and earth, and the seas and all that is in them; and in one Christ Jesus, the Son of God, who became man for our salvation; and in the Holy Ghost who proclaimed through the prophets the dispensations of God, and the advents, and the birth from a virgin, and the passion, and the resurrection from the dead, and the ascension in the flesh into heaven of the beloved Christ Jesus our Lord, and His return from the heavens in the glory of the Father to sum up all things, and to raise all flesh of the whole human race."

The doctrines selected for statement in this work are as such as contradicted Gnosticism. God the Father is the maker of the world; Jesus Christ was truly man, even in His ascension bearing the flesh of humanity.

The defence of the faith by emphasizing the witness of the churches apostolically or anciently founded, and by referring to definite statements of Christian belief commonly held, was further strengthened by the testimony of the Christian Scriptures.

The Gnostic heresy which made important the more careful organization of Christian life in the Church, and the more careful formulation of Christian truth in the Creed, led also to the determination of the Canon. Over against the list of authoritative writings drawn up by Marcion, the fathers set the books which they agreed to include in the New Testament. The earliest list of canonical scriptures is the "Muratorian Fragment," belonging probably to the latter part of the second century. Irenæus names the four Gospels. About the same time Tatian (170) was combining the four Gospels for continuous reading in his "Diatessaron." The process of discussion resulted in a list made by Athanasius which is identical with the New Testament as we have it. The acceptance of the Athanasian Canon accompanied the acceptance of Nicene Christianity.

III

Against Rivalry

The third antagonist of the Christian faith was rivalry.

The old religion of the Roman world was losing its mastery over human life because of its failure to meet certain imperative needs. It took little account of sin, except such ritual offenses as prevented the proper offering of the sacrifices. It was therefore unconcerned as to salvation. And it dealt in a very vague and uncertain way with the life to come. It was as prosaic, as practical, and as secular as politics; with which, indeed, it was so connected that political position carried religious duty with it, and whoever became a magistrate became a priest at the same time, during his term of office.

But the Roman world was dissatisfied with a religion which lacked the element of redemption. It was a part of the initial advantage of Christianity that it came as a religion of salvation from sin, and brought a definite promise of eternal life. This advantage, however, it shared with two other religions which vigorously competed with it. One of these was Mithraism, a revival of paganism; the other was Neoplatonism, a revival of philosophy.

Mithraism was already ancient in the East before it appeared in the West. Mithra, in the Vedas, was the god of light, both in the sky and in the soul, the enemy of darkness and of error. In the Avesta, he was between the good god Ormazd and the bad god Ahriman. His function was to destroy evil; he was the god of the harvest, and of victory in battle, and of the triumph of the life of man over the death of the body. All the Persians worshipped him. About the second century before Christ the Greeks of Asia Minor identified him with the Sun, and a Pergamene artist made the bas-relief which ever after served as the altar-piece of all the Mithraic shrines. Mithra, represented as a youth with Phrygian cap, and cloak blown by the wind, is slaying a sacred bull. On one side a figure with torch inverted symbolizes night, or winter, or death; on the other side a figure with torch uplifted symbolizes dawn, or spring, or life. The blood of the bull fertilizes the earth, out of which flowers and wheat are rising. Lesser reliefs along the frame show Mithra born among the rocks and adored by shepherds, and after his conquest with the bull feasting with the Sun.

The religion of Mithra admitted the worshipper to the salvation which the god had wrought. There was a baptism in the blood of a bull *(taurobolium)* which effected a new birth, concerning which was used the phrase *in æternum renatus.* There was a stated gradation of spiritual progress, an attaining of now this rank and then that, with accompanying ceremonies. For those who gained the higher privileges there was a sacrament of bread and mingled wine and water. Before the mystic bas-relief, in which the laying of the bull took the place which was occupied in Christian churches by the death upon the cross, was an altar with many lights, before which vested priests sang litanies to the sound of music. The coincidences scandalized and dismayed the Christians.

This religion, entering the Roman world in the first century with the Cilician pirates who were captured by Pompey, was carried by foreign merchants along all the lines of trade, and by foreign soldiers who served in the Roman legions along all the military roads. It appealed to traders because Mithra was a god of prosperity, and to soldiers because Mithra was a god of victory; but it appealed also to thousands of plain

71

citizens because, in the midst of a wicked world, it was a religion of righteousness, hating falsehood and iniquity, and in the midst of sorrow it promised a blessed life to come. Mithra was to descend from heaven and take with him all the faithful into joy everlasting. It made a further appeal to thoughtful and conservative people, because it proposed to include under Mithra, god of the Sun, all the other gods with all their ancient rituals.

It was this hospitality which brought about the eventual failure of Mithraism. The religion grew till it seemed about to conquer its Christian rival. The emperors liked it because with its central deity it lent itself to centralized government. But it was perceived at last that all the old religions, outworn and immoral, were returning in its train. It had had from the beginning two defects which must finally destroy it: it was a man's religion, having no place in it for women; and it was founded on faith in a god who never actually existed, but was a poetic symbol of the power of nature. Thus it waned, and disappeared late in the fourth century, leaving as a heritage to Christianity the name of Sunday for the day of the week which it agreed with the Christians in keeping holy, and the twenty-fifth of December, which it had celebrated as the birthday of the Unconquered Sun.

Neoplatonism was an endeavor to combine the philosophies as Mithraism endeavored to combine the religions. But it was a religion rather than a philosophy because it subordinates knowledge and discredited all intellectual processes, putting its faith in revelation. The current philosophies had long taught men to

despise the world of the senses,—except the philosophy of Epicurus, which the Neoplatonists hated.
Neoplatonism taught men to despise the world of
reason. It offered to uplift its disciples into a new
world, a world of revelation, wherein, all things material and even intellectual left behind, they came by
trance and ecstasy into the presence of God.

Plotinus wrote the Scriptures of Neoplatonism
in his six books called the "Enneads," that is, the
Nines. Plato he knew; Aristotle he knew; Oriental
religions he may have known, for he lived in Alexandria where the West and the East met. He said that at
the heart of the universe is the One, and with the One
is thought, and with Thought is the Soul—the world-
soul, and the individual soul. The soul lives in the
material world. It ought to be the master of the world;
but there is matter, source of all evil, in which the soul
is imprisoned. How shall it escape? This is the supreme
question, beside which all the occupations of the mind
of man are insignificant and foolish. Plotinus answered
it by saying that the escape of the soul is effected in
part by virtuous living, and in part by ascetic practices.
Thus living, putting the evil and material world away,
meditating in silence upon things divine, the soul en-
ters into communion with God. Porphyry, the chief
disciple of Plotinus, said that during the six years of
their intimate friendship the master entered four times
into this beatific state.

Porphyry, who wrote a book "Against the
Christians," hurt his cause by trying, like Mithraism, to
save the old religions. The revelation of God, he truly
held, is made in all the world; but especially, he added,

in the ancient cults with their immemorial liturgies. But the essential weakness of Neoplatonism was in the narrow range of its appeal. It addressed itself to cultivated people, and, among them, to such as had the temperament of the mystic. It was right in its insistence upon a supreme good, beyond sense, beyond reason, beyond reality, but when it endeavored to explain what that supreme good is, the plain man could not understand it.

The emperor Julian tried to substitute Neoplatonism for Christianity, but in vain. The emperor Justinian closed the doors of the Academy of Athens, and the seven philosophers, who alone represented the Neoplatonic faith, took their books and sought the hospitality of the East. Just at that time, however, an anonymous writer bearing the name of Dionysius the Areopagite, whom Paul converted at Athens, appeared at Constantinople and gained immediate acceptance. It was Neoplatonism from beginning to end. It summoned men to renounce the world, to put away from them all hindering conditions, to devote themselves to silence and meditation and solitary absorption in God. It exalted the cloistered life, and for a thousand years determined the monastic mood. It set the note of the mysticism of the saints. Thus Neoplatonism, defeated in its competition with Christianity for the allegiance of the Roman world, nevertheless profoundly affected Christianity itself.

Against Mithraism and Neoplatonism the Christian fathers defended the faith, not so much by controversy as by discriminating sympathy. They hated polytheism and idolatry and all their attendant superstitions and immoralities, and thus far they were the enemies of each of these attempts to save the gods of paganism. But the inclusive purpose of both Mithraism and Neoplatonism found in them a fraternal response. They believed in the Light which lighteth every man, and found gleams of it in all human endeavor after God. Clement and Origen were widely read in Greek literature and philosophy. Clement was a Neoplatonist. Origen was a fellow student with Plotinus in the school of Ammonius Saccas. The perception of God in all honest thought was, indeed, confined mainly to the Greek fathers. The Latins were of another mind. Tertullian, contemporary with Clement and Origen, hated all philosophy and poetry. This was in part by reason of his temperament, but also, in equal part, by reason of his ignorance. The Latin fathers were unable to read Greek. To Clement and Origen, brought up in Alexandria, the Greek mind and the Greek spirit were gifts of God. They themselves possessed them, being Greeks. And the aspiration after the unseen and ineffable, the endeavor by prayer, and pure living, and continued eager meditation, to ascend to God, was one in which they shared.

The three books which remain of the writings of Clement represent the stages through which the disciple passed in the religion of Mithra, in the religion of the Neoplatonists, in the Eleusinian mysteries— purification, initiation, revelation. Through these stages he was accustomed to lead his pupils in the Catechetical School of Alexandria. Clement's "Address to the Greeks" deals with the error and absurdity of the classic pagan religion, and shows how the greatest of the Greeks had visions of the one God, whom we see truly in the face of Jesus Christ. His "Pedagogue" is a handbook of Christian manners, describing in great detail how a Christian ought to order his life, how he should eat and drink, and furnish his house, and associate with his neighbors. His "Miscellanies" (*stromateis* = bags for bedclothes) justify the name, discussing all manner of themes without order or sequence; but the general purpose is to show the character of the true Christian, whom Clement does not hesitate to call the true Gnostic. The progress which Clement endeavored to assist in the life of the individual, he perceived in the religious history of the race. Moses prepared the Jews for Christianity; Plato prepared the Greeks. In all religions, in all good books, by all knowledge, Christ brings men to himself.

The most eminent pupil of Clement, having the same liberal spirit together with greater learning, was his successor, Origen. Origen not only exceeded the fame of his master, but attained a place in the history of theology which is equaled only by Athanasius and Augustine. He had some trouble with ecclesiastical authority, and did not get on well with the bishop, Demetrius of Alexandria. The records do not show that he was seriously at fault. He was so subjected, however, to episcopal interruption of his studies that he removed from Alexandria to Cæsarea, where he suffered martyrdom in the Decian persecution. After his death various vigorous controversies arose as to certain of his teachings. In the course of his voluminous writings he had given his opinion upon almost every possible doctrine, and it was easy to differ from him in detail. There were those who disliked what he said about the preëxistence of souls, or the plurality of worlds, or the resurrection of the flesh. He supplied the theologians for several hundred years with subjects for acrimonious debate. These circumstances hindered and prevented his ecclesiastical recognition. Neither Clement nor Origen was given the honorary degree which is denoted by the title "saint."

Nevertheless, Origen served Christianity in two remarkable and valuable ways: he was the founder of the science of Biblical criticism; he was also the founder of the science of systematic theology.

Origen was the first Christian commentator. He addressed himself through years of laborious study to the perfecting of the text of the Bible, especially of the Old Testament, comparing manuscripts, setting down the Hebrew and the various Greek versions in parallel columns, to make his great work the "Hexapla." And the Bible which he thus studied textually he also studied exegetically. He commented upon it, chapter by chapter. His method here was unfortunate, and delayed for a thousand years the investigation of the actual meaning of the Bible writers. He made everything into allegory. Thus he occupied himself not in ascertaining what the Bible says, but in reading into it his own ideas. And in this reversal of the true method of study he was followed by generations of devout readers, who instead of listening to the Bible men, prophets and apostles, insisted upon telling the apostles and prophets what they ought to mean.

Origen was at the same time the first Christian theologian. In his book "Against Celsus," he met as best he could the anti-Christian arguments of that keen antagonist, but in his "First Principles" he made the initial attempt to state in order, with due accompaniment of proof from Scripture and from reason, the doctrine of the Christian faith. From the Gnostics and the Neoplatonists he brought over into the church the idea of a theological system, a synthesis of right belief. He treated of God, one and immutable, revealing himself in the Word, begotten of the substance of the Father, co-eternal and co-substantial, yet inferior, being created. The Word, he said, came to redeem man whose soul is contending with his body. The Word, having first sent the prophets, came at last himself, taking human form. Ordinary men He redeems by the sacrifice of the cross, freeing them from bondage to the devil, and thus making it possible for them to work out their salvation from the flesh. Wise men, spiritual men, those whom like Clement he called Gnostics, He redeems by the illumination of their souls.

CHAPTER IV

THE ORGANIZATION OF RELIGION

When we seek for the beginning of definite and settled organization in the Christian church we find it not in the first or second century, but in the third, and not in the East, but in the West.

I

The Order and Function of Religion

The idea of a permanent ordering of the administration and of the worship of the Christians was excluded from the minds of the early disciples by their expectation of the speedy return of Christ. It did not occur to them to lay abiding foundations in a world which might at any moment pass away. It was necessary, indeed, to provide for local and temporary emergencies. Thus the apostles directed the selection of seven men to care for neglected widows in Jerusalem, and Paul ordained elders to hold the converts together in the cities which he visited in his missionary journeys. Such titles appear as bishops, priests, and deacons, pastors, prophets, teachers, and evangelists. But the records give the impression of informality, and of a tentative adjustment to meet immediate needs.

Ignatius, it is true, urges obedience to bishops, but what he has in mind seems to be a loyalty to the local minister in the face of divisive individualism. Irenæus, indeed, attaches much importance to bishops, but chiefly as persons to whom inquirers or doubters may be referred for information as to the faith. It is a curious story which is told of the way in which Demetrius, bishop of Alexandria in the time of Origen, came to his position. From time immemorial the pastors of the twelve city parishes had elected a bishop. But Bishop Julian, on his deathbed, had a vision of a man who should be his successor, coming to him with a present of grapes; and as he waked there came out of the country, bringing grapes, the peasant Demetrius, with his wife. He was accordingly made bishop without consulting the college of presbyters, and proved to be a masterful one, as Origen discovered to his cost.

Thus we proceed, down the line of saints and confessors, till we come, in the middle of the third century, to Cyprian. He was the father of ecclesiastics as Origen was the father of theologians.

Cyprian had the spirit of the West, where men were interested in practical suggestion of administration. He had been a lawyer before he became a bishop. The eminent men of the church in the East were successors of the Greek philosophers. Justin, as we have seen, wore his philosopher's cloak to the day of his martyrdom. Irenæus and Clement and Origen taught a Christian philosophy. These men and their disciples delighted in the study of theological problems. The Nicene Creed was framed in the East. There were theologians in the West, but they cared more for tradition than they did for speculation. But the eminent men of the West were successors of the Latin statesmen. Their gift was for order and rule. They hated confusion. They prized efficiency. Accordingly, while their brethren in the East were discussing and establishing the formulation of Christian thought in the creed, these men were discussing and establishing the organization of Christian life in the church.

The progress of this ecclesiastical organization appears in a series of protests. It was vigorously opposed by the Montanists, by the Novatians, and by the Donatists.

The Montanists first appeared in Phrygia in the middle of the second century when Montanus began to proclaim the nearness of the Second Coming of Christ, and to summon Christians to prepare for it by a return to primitive simplicity and severity of life. Montanus was a prophet.

In the list of ministerial officers which St. Paul gives in the First Epistle to the Corinthians (XII, 28) the prophets are the second order: "first apostles, secondarily prophets." They are mentioned in the Te Deum where the "goodly fellowship of the Prophets" follows the "glorious company of the Apostles"; and it is to the Christian teachers rather than to men of the Old Testament that reference is made in the phrase, "who hast built Thy Church upon the foundation of the Apostles and Prophets." They rose up, like the Old Testament prophets, at the direct call of God, having no official appointment. They asked no permission of any man. What they spoke was by inspiration from on high. Wandering from place to place, speaking unbidden in the Christian assemblies to which they came, they represented all that was free and spontaneous and informal in primitive Christianity. They expressed themselves frankly and without mitigation regarding whatever they found amiss.

Montanus and his followers found things seriously amiss in two respects.

They perceived the beginning of secularism. There were Christians who were in the church because they had been brought up in it; and others who had come because their friends or relatives were in it. Upon these Christians the burden of the rigorous life of the gospel lay rather lightly. Moreover, as the first novelty of the Christian movement passed, the distinction, at first so sharp, between the church and the world grew gradually obscure. Many of the Christians were content to have it so. They were adjusting themselves to their environment. They perceived that it was prudent to make some reasonable compromise, and to concede to common custom some matters about which it seemed hardly necessary to contend.

For example, the emperor Severus gave a donative to the army; every man received a piece of money.

On this occasion, the soldiers in Africa adorned their heads with wreaths. One Christian soldier refused to wear a wreath. The incident was excitedly discussed; the soldier, meanwhile, being degraded from the ranks and put in prison. Most of the Christians condemned the soldier. The Montanists praised him.

At the same time, while excellent reasons might be shown for a sensible secularism, it was plain that the main contention of the Montanists was right. There was a relaxing of discipline, a lowering of Christian standards of conduct, an increasing concession to the world. Against all this the Montanists protested. Montanus, speaking by the Holy Ghost, called his brethren to fasting, to strictness, even to martyrdom. Looking for the great and dreadful day of the Lord; he tried to purify the church.

The Montanists perceived the beginning not only of secularism, but of formalism. Emphasis was being put on order, and authority, and regularity. A difference was being made between the clergy and the laity. There were now appointed persons to whom were given all the old rights of free speech and free prayer. Other people were expected to keep silence. The behavior of the congregation of Corinth, where, as St. Paul said, when they came together every one had a psalm, a doctrine, a tongue, or an interpretation, was now regarded as scandalous. To the Montanists, it was the ideal of Christian conduct. They felt that any restraint of it was a restraint of the Holy Spirit. They were the Quakers of the early church. The Montanists declined to be bound by the disciplinary regulations. They defied the new distinction between the presbyter and the people. They so insisted on their right to speak in meeting, and so exercised that right in season and out of season, that the whole ministry of preaching came under suspicion. Over against the growing system of canons and rubrics, they opposed the primitive simplicity of apostolic religion.

The most distinguished Western Montanist was Tertullian. He was born and brought up in Carthage, the son of a centurion. These two facts affected his whole life.

In Carthage, the life of the senses was encouraged under the patronage of pagan religion. Tertullian was nurtured in it, harmed by it, and converted out of it, and thereafter he hated it with the vigorous hatred of reaction. He had been a sinner. He knew by hard experience what the world was. He saw it everyday, cruel and foul dominated by the devil. The Montanist teaching appealed, therefore, to his whole soul: the church must have no commerce with the world.

As the son of a soldier, Tertullian was a fighter. His whole life, after his conversion, was continuous controversy. He fought that pagan world which the Christian fathers of Alexandria regarded so kindly. He denounced its sins, he scorned its religion, he had no use even for its philosophy. What, he said, has the Church to do with the Academy? What kinship is there between Christ and Plato? It was Tertullian who first clearly sounded the note of the unhappy antagonism between the church and the learning of the world. He set faith over against reason, and cried, "It is certain because it is impossible!"

Tertullian fought the church also. He was the enemy of all worldly Christians, whom he desired to see put out of the church and kept out. He was the Hammer of Heretics. He wrote five books "Against Marcion." Pontus, he says at the beginning of this discussion, is inhabited by the fiercest nations, who have no fixed abode, and no morals. The dead bodies of their parents they cut up with their sheep, and devour at their feasts. Their women prefer war to marriage. The sky of Pontus is always cloudy, and the wind always from the north; all the rivers are blocked with ice. Nothing, however, in Pontus is so barbarous and sad as the fact that Marcion was born there.

Finally, Tertullian turned this zeal for invective against the ecclesiastical authorities, whom he rebuked for their conventionalism, for their indifference, and for the manner in which they magnified their office. "Are not we laymen priests also?" he cried. Thus he separated himself from the bishops and became identified with Montanism; which, refused and expelled, had now become a society outside the church.

The Novatians came into existence by reason of the controversy which arose after the Decian persecutions. When the distresses were over, and the church resumed its normal life, there appeared great numbers of lapsed brethren. Some who had not actually burned incense on pagan altars had purchased certificates from the magistrates stating that they had done so; others who had burned incense and then repented had papers signed by martyrs in prison stating that they had been absolved, or ought to be absolved. The whole church was in confusion.

Under the circumstances, churchmen took two sides. Some were temperamentally or doctrinally of a liberal spirit, and were in favor of treating the lapsed gently. The absolution of the martyrs was indeed to be set aside as subversive of all discipline, but the lapsed, after proper penance and probation were to be restored to the community of the church. Others, who were doctrinally or temperamentally austere, were disposed to deal with the lapsed severely. They denied the right of absolution not only to the martyrs, but to the bishops. Sin after baptism, they said, has no forgiveness in this world.

The severe party took its name from Novatian, who having failed of election to the bishopric of Rome was thereupon elected to that office by his friends. Thus the Novatians became a sect. The most eminent opponent of the Novatians was Cyprian.

Cyprian had been the most eloquent orator in Carthage, at a time when oratory was greatly esteemed. A man of wealth and position, he had given up his prospects, and even his property, to become a Christian. He had entered the ministry, and shortly after, when the bishop died, the Christian people by popular acclaim had called him to be bishop. When the Decian persecution began, Cyprian had retired into the country, deeming it more important for the church that its leaders should continue to lead than that they should give their lives in martyrdom. That this flight was in fact dictated rather by prudence than by fear, he proved when the persecution was renewed by Valerian. He met the Roman officers with all confidence, proclaimed himself a Christian and a bishop, and was beheaded.

To an administrative mind like that of Cyprian the Novatian protest presented two questions: as to the right of the church to absolve, and as to the right of the churchmen to secede.

The question as to the right of the church to absolve he answered in the affirmative. Against those who held that the church is a society of saints, out of which all offenders must be permanently expelled, he held that the church is properly composed of those who are striving, however unsuccessfully, after perfection, and that the purpose of the Christian fraternity is to assist such striving persons. The church, he said, may determine its own conditions of membership, and may administer discipline according to its own discretion. The church, following Christ's commission, may forgive sins. That this position represented the general mind of Christendom is witnessed by the phrase "the forgiveness of sins," as it stood thereafter in the ancient creeds. It follows "the holy Catholic Church," the "one Catholic and Apostolic Church," and is the expression of one of its functions. It declares that the forgiveness of sins is to be sought in the church, and that the church is holy in spite of the presence of sinners. At the same time the effect was to emphasize the nature of the church as a society held together by the bonds of organization, and including saints and sinners, as opposed to the idea of a church invisible and spiritual, a company of faithful people, to which they belonged, and they only, who were unfailingly loyal to Jesus Christ.

The question as to the right of churchmen to secede, Cyprian answered in the negative. The Novatians had separated themselves from the general society. Declining to obey bishops regularly appointed, and electing rival bishops, they had their own complete independent organization, their own buildings, ministry and sacraments. To the Latin mind, accustomed to the order of the empire, this was a state of things which must not be permitted to continue. Indeed, it was plain to all reflective persons that a divided Christendom, broken into fragments, disagreeing and competing, church against church, could not maintain itself against the hostile world. It was a practical matter. The doctrine which was essentially involved in it was no more ecclesiastical, or even religious, than the doctrine involved in the American Civil War. It was a matter of policy: Shall we be a nation, or shall we be a federation of states, from which any state may withdraw at will? Shall we be a church, or shall we be a federation of churches, from which any company of persons, on the ground of disagreement regarding faith or discipline, may quietly secede?

The question arose in the case of Novatians and other separated persons who had been baptized by the ministers of their sect, and now desired to become members of the historic church: ought they to be rebaptized? Cyprian took the extreme position. He would recognize no validity whatever in the acts of the seceded churches. In this he was not supported by the general opinion. It was commonly felt that, however great the evil of secession, the wise policy of centralization was pushed too far when it thus discredited the ministry of men whose chief fault was that they were more intent than their neighbors upon the purity of the church. It was agreed against Cyprian that the returning Novatians need not be baptized again.

But a book which Cyprian wrote on the general subject, the "Unity of the Catholic Church," made a profound and lasting impression. This book is related to the ecclesiastical progress of the early church as the Nicene Creed is related to its theological progress. Out of long confusion and experiment, and in the midst of conditions which were compelling a definition of the church, Cyprian made a clear statement. It did not appear to him a novel statement, though it had no warrant in the New Testament; neither did it seem original to his contemporaries, for they had been gradually coming to a like conclusion. Nevertheless, it introduced into Christian history a proposition as new and as radical as that which was afterwards presented on the other side by Luther. Luther declared that all men are in need of the grace of God, without which they cannot be saved, and that this grace comes straight from God, without the mediation of any priest or rite, into the heart of the individual. That doctrine began the Reformation and the era in which we live, wherein the unit is the individual. Cyprian declared that all men are in need of the grace of God, without which they cannot be saved, and that this grace is to be had only in the church, into which it comes by the medium of the bishop, who derives it from the apostles.

Ignatius had exalted the bishop as the head of the Christian community, who is to be obeyed as the soldiers obey their captain. Irenæus had exalted him as the arbiter in disputes about the faith, having received the tradition of the fathers. Cyprian brought at last to the episcopal office the sanction of divine right. Surrounded as the Christians were by universal paganism, they breathed in out of the air the idea of the bishop as a sacrificing priest, and the idea of God as limiting His benediction to the faithful. These ideas Cyprian clearly enunciated. To him the Novatians and other separatists were like men swimming in the rising waters of the flood: their only sure salvation was to get aboard the ark, the church.

A third protest which marks the further progress of ecclesiastical organization was made by the Donatists. They came into being in consequence of the persecution under Diocletian, as the Novatians had come into being in consequence of the persecution under Decius. The Diocletian persecution had been directed mainly against the clergy, who were required to surrender the church books. When peace was restored, the ecclesiastical standing of the clergy who had made this surrender was called in question. Had the traditor, by the fact of his treachery, forfeited his orders? The Novatians had insisted that no libellatic, who had procured a paper certifying that he had offered incense, could be restored to the means of grace: he had committed a sin beyond forgiveness. Now the Donatists insisted that no traditor, no clergyman who had give up the sacred books, could validly administer the means of grace.

As in the case of the Montanists and Novatians the debate centred in Carthage. Cæcilian the archdeacon had been elected and duly consecrated bishop of that city. But he had enemies. Two of them were trustees of the funds of the diocese, whom Cæcilian had discovered to be dishonest. One was the lady Lucilla whom Cæcilian had rebuked for her habit of bringing to church a bone of a martyr and kissing it before receiving the bread and wine. Another was Donatus, the bishop of a neighboring diocese. Thus, as in the case of the Novatians, personal animosities confused discussion. Donatus and his friends declared that Cæcilian had been consecrated by a traditor, and that his consecration was no consecration, and they proceeded to put a rival bishop in his place.

Whatever were the rights and wrongs of the matter, the Donatists stood for the purity of the church. They insisted that the supreme quality of the minister is derived not from his office, but from his character. They did not demand an impossible perfection, but they held that certain sins, of which apostasy was one, destroyed the reality of the ministry. They maintained that the sacraments administered by bad men are invalid. An unholy ministry, they said, cannot communicate to men the grace of God. Their baptism is no baptism; their eucharist is no eucharist.

Against this position the church in general maintained that such a theory made all the sacraments uncertain. Nobody could tell whether at the moment of administration the bishop or presbyter or deacon was good enough, or not. The church held that the grace of God is independent of the minister.

The Donatists appealed to Constantine shortly after his conversion, and he appointed a committee of bishops to hear their case. The decision was adverse to the plaintiffs, and they appealed again, and Constantine called a conference at Arles (314), interesting to us as having been attended by three British bishops. This council confirmed the decision against the Donatists. Thereupon they rebelled not only against the church, but against the state. They attracted to themselves those who were fanatical in their religion and revolutionary in their politics. A socialistic strain was added to their heresy and schism. Vagrants and brigands came to their assistance, bringing clubs with which they defaced the churches and attacked the persons of the orthodox. The church and the state replied with corresponding violence. At last, the original grievance was forgotten in the host of new ones.

Meanwhile, the answers which were given to these various Protestants—Montanist, Novatian, and Donatist—had determined the organization of the church. Against the protest of the Novatians, a line had been drawn between the church and all separated Christian communities, who were denied the right of secession, and were informed that if they seceded they were cut off from the means of grace. Against the protest of the Donatists, a line was drawn between the old idea of a personal ministry whose efficiency depended on character and the new idea of an official ministry whose efficiency depended on proper appointment.

At the same time it is plain that in the middle of the third century, in the time of Cyprian, the ministers were bishops, priests and deacons. Any congregational or presbyterian experiments which may have been tried had failed. The primacy of the bishops of Rome was only beginning to appear. There was a pope in Carthage and a pope in Alexandria as well as a pope in Rome. These prelates already interfered with the primitive equality and independence of the bishops. But none of them controlled the general church.

II

Forms of Worship

While the church in the West was thus determining the order and function of the ministry, the church in the East was developing and enriching the forms of worship. The earliest liturgies are in Greek; in which language St. Paul wrote to the church in Rome, and St. Clement of Rome wrote from that city to the church in Corinth. The church in Italy was a Greek mission. When Latin liturgies begin to appear, they are translations, with some changes, from the Greek.

A description of a church building in the tenth book of the "Ecclesiastical History" of Eusebius, and a complete service of the administration of the Holy Communion in the eighth book of the "Apostolic Constitutions," enable us to transport ourselves in imagination into the early years of the fourth century and to take part in the prayers and praises of our brethren of that day.

The Diocletian persecution, beginning with the demolition of the great church of Nicomedia and addressing itself to the general destruction of church buildings, was followed by a period of architectural restoration. Thus at Tyre, in 315, Bishop Paulinus built a new and splendid church on the site which had been strewn with the ruins of the old. On the occasion of the consecration of this church, Bishop Eusebius of Cæsarea preached the sermon, and afterwards published it in his history. In the course of the sermon he so referred to various parts of the church as to direct not only the eyes of the congregation, but even the minds of remote readers to the general look of things.

Tyre, in 315, is still a pagan city. The Christian congregation going to service pass pagan temples, and recognized pagan neighbors who took an enthusiastic part in pulling down the old church and would be glad to visit the same zeal upon the new. All the adult Christians know by bitter experience the meaning of persecution. The first sight which we get of the church shows the high wall which stands about it, facing the street. This is a barrier of stone a hundred and twenty-nine feet in breadth, and two hundred and twenty-two in length. It is lofty enough to afford seclusion, and stout enough to serve for defence in case of another pagan assault. Passing through a great gate, made splendid to attract the eyes of strangers to the faith, we enter a large quadrangle, open to the sky, having pillared porticoes on the four sides, and in the midst a fountain of water. Here we wash our hands before proceeding into the church, symbolizing the importance of a pure heart. In the latticed porches are people who are under penance. They are suffering the worst punishment known at that day to Christian men, being forbidden to go to church. They stand there in the vestibule, asking our prayers.

The church has three doors, a greater in the midst, a lesser on each side. The middle door is adorned with plates of brass. The side doors lead into the side aisles between the outer walls and pillars which uphold the roof. The pillars are of rose-colored granite, the ceiling is of cedar; between the pillars and the walls are galleries. Entering by the middle door, we stand in an inner vestibule, parted by a low barrier from the nave. Here are strangers, who have come from curiosity to see the church or hear the sermon; and catechumens who are preparing for baptism and confirmation; and persons of disordered minds, "entangled by contrary qualities," to whom the church extends a certain perplexed hospitality. Young deacons and deaconesses in white gowns are moving about to see that all the men and women are in order. In the midst of the nave is a platform for readers and singers. The floor is of marble. Texts of Scripture, and portraits of the emperor or of the bishop are painted on the walls.

The chancel is parted from the nave by a screen of carved and latticed wood, and has a curtain hanging at the door, ready to be drawn in the more solemn moments of the service. Beyond the screen is the altar, standing in the middle of the apse. It is a table of wood covered with rich tapestry, having as yet no cross upon it, but adorned with gold and silver cups and bowls and lighted with silver lamps. Behind the altar is the high seat of the bishop, with seats on either side for the clergy. To the right of the chancel is a room for the preparation of the bread and wine; to the left is a room for the clergy.

After the record of the words of institution, as uttered by our Lord at the Last Supper, in the First Epistle to the Corinthians and in the Synoptic Gospels, the earliest of our liturgy sentences appear in the Canons of Hippolytus, early in the third century. The third canon gives these versicles and responses:—

> *Let the bishop say:* The Lord be with you all.
> *Let the people reply:* And with thy spirit.
> *Let him say:* Lift up your hearts.
> *Answer:* We lift them up unto the Lord.
> *Bishop:* Let us give thanks unto the Lord.
> *Answer:* It is meet and right so to do.

The nineteenth canon gives the words of distribution:—

Let the deacon bring the oblation to the bishop. And he shall give thanks over a loaf, because it is the symbol of the flesh of Christ, and over a chalice of wine because it is the blood of Christ which was outpoured for all that believe in him, and over milk and honey mixed, for the fulfilling of the promise unto the fathers: for he hath said, "I will give unto you a land flowing with milk and honey." And when the bishop has now broken the bread, let him give a fragment to every one of them, saying, "This is the bread of heaven, the body of Jesus Christ." Let him also that receives say, "Amen." And if there be not a presbyter present, let the deacons take the chalice and stand in fair order, and give them the blood of Jesus Christ our Lord, and the milk and honey. And let him that giveth the chalice say, "This is the blood of Jesus Christ our Lord." Let him also that receives again say, "Amen."

In the middle of the fourth century, the Catechetical Lectures of Cyril of Jerusalem and the Sacramentary of Serapion describe the order of the eucharistic service and give the words of some of the prayers.

Cyril instructs his confirmation class in the order and meaning of the Holy Communion. The deacon, he says, gives the priest water to wash his hands; the men of the congregation greet the men, and the women greet the women, with the kiss of peace. Then the priest cries aloud, "Lift up your hearts," and you answer, "We lift them up unto the Lord." The priest says, "It is meet and right." A long thanksgiving follows, culminating in the ascription, "Holy, holy, holy is the Lord of Sabaoth." No mention is made of the words of institution; perhaps kept secret till the catechumen is actually admitted to the Sacrament. But there is a prayer for the descent of the Holy Spirit that he may make the bread the body of Christ, and the wine the blood of Christ. Prayers are made for the living and for the dead, ending with the Lord's Prayer. Then the priest cries, "Holy things to holy persons," and you say, "One is holy, one is the Lord, even Jesus Christ." Cyril tells them to receive the bread, "making the left hand a throne for the right." The service ends with renewed prayer and thanksgiving.

Serapion begins with, "It is meet and right," and gives the actual words of the service as he said it, in the middle of the fourth century in his diocese in the Delta of the Nile. A long thanksgiving rises to the "Holy, holy, holy, Lord of Sabaoth, full is heaven and the earth of thy glory." The words of institution are recited. "The Lord Jesus Christ, in the night in which He was betrayed, took bread, and brake and gave to His disciples, saying, Take and eat; this is my body which is being broken for you. Wherefore we also making the likeness of the death have offered the bread, and we beseech thee through this sacrifice be reconciled to all of us, and be merciful, O God of truth. And as this bread had been scattered on the top of the mountains and, gathered together, came to be one, so also gather together thy holy church out of every nation and every country and city and village and house, and make one living Catholic Church." Similarly, the wine is offered. An invocation of the Holy Spirit follows, then intercessions. Then the people receive the bread and wine.

To the same period belongs the liturgy named from St. Clement of Rome in the Apostolic Constitutions. The name is of no historic significance, and the attributing of the whole through Clement to the apostles is only a literary device; the value of the account for us is that it preserves not only the order but the words of the service of the fourth century. Harnack's date for the Apostolic Constitutions is about 340, but the liturgy here contained is neither original nor novel. It is a fair conjecture that after this manner the service was said in that church in Tyre which the sermon of Eusebius enables us to visit.

Passing, then, into the nave, and joining the company of the faithful who are there assembled, the men on one side and the women on the other, we hear

the reader beginning the service from the high platform in the midst. He reads two lessons from the Old
Testament; then a single voice sings several psalms, the
people joining "at the conclusion of the verses"; then
is read a passage from an epistle, and then a passage
from a gospel. And while the gospel is read all the
clergy and people "stand up in great silence." Sermons
follow, "Let the presbyters one by one, not all together, exhort the people, and the bishop in the last
place, as being the commander." The preacher stands
on the raised platform, or on the chancel step. The
deacons move about and "oversee the people, that
nobody may whisper, nor slumber, nor laugh, nor
nod." Then the inner vestibule is cleared. First the
hearers, strangers, unbelievers, are dismissed; then the
catechumens, then the energumens—the crazy people—then the penitents go out, each group dismissed
in order after prayer and blessing. Only the faithful, the
communicants, remain; among them the children who
are assembled at the reading desk under the care of a
deacon.

The service begins again with a long prayer for
Christ's Church militant. The kiss of peace is given.
The officiating priests wash their hands. The deacons
bring the bread and wine to the Lord's table. Two of
them, on each side of the altar, having fans of peacock
feathers, drive away the flies. The celebrant puts on a
shining garment. Then standing at the altar, and making the sign of the cross, he says, "The grace of Almighty God, and the love of our Lord Jesus Christ,
and the fellowship of the Holy Ghost, be with you all."
We reply, "And with thy spirit." "Lift up your mind."

99

"We lift it up unto the Lord." "Let us give thanks to the Lord." "It is meet and right so to do." "It is very meet and right," the priest repeats, "to sing praise unto thee." And praises follow, at great length, for all the blessings of creation, until the worshippers join their voices with the angels and archangels, crying, "Holy, holy, holy, Lord God of hosts, heaven and earth are full of His glory. Blessed be thou forever. Amen."

Again the praises are renewed for all the blessings of salvation, coming presently to the night when He who was betrayed took bread, and brake it, and poured the wine and gave it to His disciples. Long intercessions follow, till the bishop cries, "Holy things to holy persons," and the people answer, "There is one that is holy, there is one Lord, one Jesus Christ, blessed forever to the glory of God the Father. Glory to God in the highest, and on earth peace, good-will toward men. Hosanna to the Son of David! Blessed be He that cometh in the name of the Lord. Hosanna in the highest!"

Then the clergy partake of the bread and wine and afterward the people in order; the ministrant saying, "The body of Christ," "The blood of Christ, the cup of life," to which we reply, "Amen." There is a prayer of dedication, and a prayer of benediction; after which the deacon cries, "Depart in peace."

CHAPTER V

THE ARIAN DEBATE

I

The Conversion of Constantine

Constantine, being the imperial ruler of Britain and Gaul, and Maxentius, being the imperial ruler of Italy, Spain, and Roman Africa, the two fell to fighting for undivided power. Down came Constantine out of Britain; in Gaul he reinforced his army; he crossed the Alps; at Verona he won a victory; and finally, at the Milvian Bridge over the Tiber, he found Maxentius holding the road to Rome. The soldiers of Constantine forced the soldiers of Maxentius back into the river, and Maxentius himself was drowned.

It was on his way to this decisive battle that Constantine was suddenly converted.

Our knowledge of the event comes mainly from Eusebius of Cæsarea, the preacher of the sermon at the consecration of the church in Tyre, who was informed by Constantine himself. On a day in October, 312, Constantine with his army was making his difficult way over the Alps. In the blaze of noon, "he saw with his own eyes," says Eusebius, "the trophy of a cross of light in the heavens, above the brightness of the sun, and bearing the inscription, 'By this conquer' (τοῦτω νίκα)." That night Christ appeared in a dream and told him to make a likeness of the celestial cross as a protection against his enemies. This he did in the form of a monogram of the first two letters of the name Christ in Greek (☧), and under banners and behind shields thus emblazoned he marched to victory.

That the course of history has been determined on several occasions by the experience of a vision is a phenomenon which is substantially attested. Saul of Tarsus saw a strange sight on the road to Damascus, and was changed thereby from a purpose to persecute the Christians to a position of singularly influential leadership among them. Augustine heard a sound of words at Milan which suddenly brought him out of indifference and doubt into a faith which mightily affected Christian theology for a thousand years, and affects it still.

A vision however, is only part a matter of the senses. Whatever the external facts may be, the determining sight is seen with the eyes of the mind, and the determining words are heard with the hearing of the mind. And the mind sees and hears what it brings of sight and hearing. And this depends on the preparation of previous thought and experience. So it was in Saul. The vision seemed as sudden as a flash of lightning; but the suddenness of lightning is only in appearance, it is the result of a long and gradual assembling of forces. The whole life of Saul had made him ready for that day. So it was with Constantine.

Diocletian, in his reorganization of the empire, had found himself confronted by the Christians. They made up one twelfth of the population, and their influence was out of all proportion to their number. They were constantly enlisting the allegiance of men of outstanding character and ability. It was plain to the emperor that he must either be the head of the Christian Church or its destroyer. He resolved to destroy it.

With this resolution the father of Constantine was not in sympathy. Constantius took such part in the general persecution as the necessities of his position demanded, but in his portion of the empire the campaign was not carried on with rigor. The young prince, his son, shared his father's counsels, and partook of his spirit.

The event had revealed the folly of Diocletian, and had justified the wisdom of Constantius. It had proved, by the hard test of persecution, that the church could not be destroyed. The alternative, then, was alliance. He who would be master of Rome,—so it appeared to the clear mind of Constantine,—must have the Christians on his side.

With these thoughts in his heart, at a critical moment in his life, on the eve of a battle the object of which was to gain the Roman throne, Constantine saw a shining object in the sky which he perceived to be the Cross of Christ.

The conversion of Constantine was at the same time a victory for Christianity and a defeat. The new religion triumphed with the converted emperor. The edict of toleration which was issued in 313 put a definite end to persecution. Thenceforth the Roman world which had been officially pagan was officially Christian. But it was like the triumph of the Romans over the Greeks, wherein the Romans held the power of position, but the Greeks retained the power of influence. The world against which the saints had protested came into alliance with the church. The current standards of life lowered the Christian standards. The current philosophy affected the Christian theology.

We stand with Constantine where two rivers meet. One is the Christian river, having its rise in Judaism, bringing down Jewish and Christian elements together. The other is the pagan river, formed from a hundred contributory streams, bringing myths and legends, ceremonies of worship, mysteries, gods and goddesses, ancient customs, ancient interpretations of the world. At this point the rivers join to form the Church Catholic, from this moment a world of religion, Christian and pagan, having its source no longer in Jerusalem and in Antioch alone, but in the springs of all the hills of history, and in the brooks which flow though all the valleys of the past. The conversion of Constantine diverted not only the Jordan and the Orontes, but the Euphrates and the Tigris, and the Nile, the Danube and the Rhine, and made them flow into the channel of the Tiber.

II
The Council of Nicaea

The first rush of the new current endangered not only the morals but the essential beliefs of Christians. It was by no accidental coincidence that the Edict of Toleration was speedily followed by the Arian Debate.

The central assertion of all advanced philosophy and religion is the assertion of the unity of God. In the fourth century it was a commonplace of educated thought. Behind the gods was God.

But pagan philosophers were denying either the personality or the presence of God. The Epicureans and the Stoics denied His personality, making Him identical with Chance or Fate, and the Gnostics and the Neoplatonists were denying His presence, conceiving of Him as infinitely removed from the affairs of the world. Pagan priests were indeed ministering to the instinct which craves relationship with God. Mithraism was providing in Mithra a mediator between God and man. But Mithra was a celestial figure whose only dwelling was in a Persian dream. He had no actual existence.

The characteristic assertion of Christianity was the declaration of the divinity of Christ. Here, they said, is the true bond of union between God and man, in Him who is at the same time God and man.

The first task of Christian theologians had been that of affirmation: thus they had met the Ebionites, who denied the divinity of Jesus, and maintained that he was only a man like us. And thus they had met the Docetics, who denied the humanity of Jesus, holding that his human form and life were not in reality but only in appearance. These affirmations they based, without much discussion, on the revelation contained in Holy Scripture.

But the task of affirmation was followed of necessity by the task of interpretation. Admitting that the Scriptures assert the divinity of Christ, how, then, is the divine Christ related to the one only God? The Sabellians explained the relation as consisting in distinction of activity. When we think of God as the maker and maintainer of the universe, we call Him the Father; when we think of Him as in Christ for the redemption of mankind, we call Him the Son. God is eternally one and the same, but we speak of Him under different names. Against this explanation, however, there was general protest. Conservative theologians held that it destroyed the Christian religion by destroying the reality of Christ. Christ, according to this doctrine, was absorbed in God.

The discussion was at this stage of progress, with Sabellianism in common disfavor, when a clergyman in Alexandria publicly accused his bishop of holding the Sabellian heresy. The accusing clergyman was Arius, the rector of the Church of Baucalis, the largest in the city. He was sixty years of age, dignified in appearance, austere, and blameless in life, learned, eloquent and pious, the most popular of the Alexandrian clergy. The Son, said Arius, is not—as Bishop Alexander and the Sabellians falsely affirm—identical with the Father. How can a son be identical with a father? There is one God, the Father, from whom the Son is derived, and to whom the Son is inferior. The Father is the Creator, eternally existing, before all time; the Son is created—there was a time (if we may use the word "time" of conditions so infinitely remote)—there was a time when He was not.

Thus over against the endeavor of the Sabellians to reconcile the divinity of Christ with the unity of God by identification, appeared the endeavor of the Arians to reconcile the divinity of Christ with the unity of God by distinction.

Immediately the church in Alexandria was divided into two contending parties, some siding with Alexander, some with Arius. Alexander appealed to his neighbors, the bishops of Egypt, summoning a council by whose action Arius was excommunicated. Arius appealed to his friends among the bishops of Syria: Eusebius of Cæsarea, Eusebius of Nicomedia, influential persons in the Court of Constantine. By them he was sustained.

The subtlety of the question was equalled only by the fury with which it was discussed. The debate was conducted with the violence of a political convention. Everybody entered into it. Men who met to transact business neglected their bargaining to talk theology. If one said to the baker, "How much is the loaf?" he would answer, "The Son is subordinate to the Father." If one sent a servant on an errand, he would reply, "The Son arose out of nothing." Arius put his doctrine into verse, to popular tunes, and it was sung and whistled in the streets. The arguments were punctuated with fists and clubs.

The news of this dissension disturbed the Christian emperor. Hoping by his espousal of Christianity to unify the empire, he was distressed to find that the Christians were themselves divided. He wrote to Alexander and to Arius, with a natural misunderstanding of the seriousness of the matter, and urged them to be reconciled and keep the peace. Believe in God, he said, and do not disturb yourselves concerning questions which no man can answer. But the letter did no good; the strife continued and increased. At last the emperor, to regain peace, determined upon the wise expedient of a free and representative assembly. He would have a meeting and conference of the chief men of the Christian religion.

Thus was convened, in the early summer of 325, the Council of Nicæa.

Asia Minor, bounded on the north by the Black Sea and on the west by the Ægean, holds between the two, at its northwest corner, the Sea of Marmora,—the Propontis,—connected with the Black Sea by the Bosphorus, and with the Ægean by the Hellespont. Opening into the Propontis from the east are a bay and a lake. On the bay is Nicomedia, then the capital of the empire of the East, and the residence of Constantine; on the lake is Nicæa.

Over the long roads, from all directions, borne in conveyances provided by the emperor, came the bishops. The number of them is uncertain, though tradition finally placed it at three hundred and eighteen, attracted by the coincidence with the number of the armed servants whom Abraham took to rout the invading kings. Most of them were from the East; partly because the place of meeting was in that region, but partly also because the church was still an Eastern Church. The West was missionary ground. Moreover, the subject of discussion was congenial with the Eastern mind; it was foreign to the practical interests of the West. The council was essentially an Eastern conference. The discussions were carried on in Greek; the resulting creed was not only in Greek, but its distinctive words were found afterwards to be almost incapable of translation into Latin.

Indeed, of the three hundred bishops, only five are known to have come from Latin Christendom: from Spain one—Hosius of Cordova, the emperor's "chaplain" in the West; from Carthage one—Cæcilian, who had contended with the Donatists; one from Calabria, one from Gaul, one from Pannonia.

But the Westerns were not missed in the throng of Easterns. From the cities which Paul had evangelized came the bishops of Greece and Asia Minor. One was Spyridion of Cyprus, a shepherd bishop, who in the intervals of his episcopal duties still watched his flock; a simple, homely man, whose embalmed body is to this day carried twice a year about the streets of Corfu in procession; one may still look upon the hands which signed the Nicene Creed. Another was Acesius,

109

a stout separatist, who believed that only he and a few like-minded with him would be saved, to whom Constantine is reported to have said, "Acesius, plant a ladder and climb up into heaven by yourself." To this a pleasant legend adds St. Nicholas of Myra, patron of the festivities of Christmas, even Santa Claus himself, who appears in an ancient picture of the council in the act of giving Arius a great box on the ear.

From Syria came Eusebius of Cæsarea, the emperor's Eastern "chaplain," a great prelate and a fair historian, afterwards biographer of Constantine; and Eusebius of Nicomedia, and Eustathius of Antioch, and Bishop John from Persia; and Bishop Jacob of Mesopotamia, who had been a hermit, and still wore his cloak of goat's hair.

From Egypt came Potammon and Paphnutius, each of whom had lost an eye in the Diocletian persecution. Indeed, many of the bishops bore the honorable marks of torture. From Alexandria came the bishop, Alexander, bringing with him as chaplain and secretary a young deacon, named Athanasius. Also came the minister of the parish of Baucalis, the heretic Arius.

In the place of meeting long benches were set against the walls on either side, upon which sat the bishops with their attendant clergy. In the middle of the room upon a chair lay a copy of the Gospels, a symbol of the presence of Him in whose name and for whose honor they were assembled. At the end of the room was a seat for the emperor. Silence was called as he approached; all rose as he entered. They said afterward that he looked like an angel from heaven. Indeed, to any eyes the face and figure of Constantine fitted his high position. He was tall and stalwart; his beard was short, his hair fell upon his shoulders; his purple robe of silk embroidered with gold and pearls; he wore his crown; his eyes, they said, flashed like the eyes of a lion. He seemed as much impressed by the situation as they were, being at first doubtful whether to stand or sit, till they beckoned to him to be seated. A speech of welcome and gratitude was made, a gracious response was returned, and the sessions of the council were formally begun.

How long the fathers sat in conference is not known; neither is there any satisfactory record of the progress of the debate.

It is remembered that early in the proceedings the emperor brought in a package of letters, and caused a fire to be made in the brazier in the hall, and burned the letters in the presence of the bishops. These, he said, are communications which you have sent to me making complaints and accusations one against another. He begged them to be brotherly, to put their bickering aside, and cultivate the virtues of peace.

As regards to the main purpose of their meeting, however, they seem to have been, for the most part, agreed. They found the doctrines of Arius novel and objectionable. It is said that when some of the songs of Arius were recited to the council, the bishops clapped their hands over their ears, and shut their eyes. Eusebius of Nicomedia presented a creed setting forth the Arian ideas, and it was torn in pieces. Arius appeared to have few friends.

When it came, however, to the formulation of an acceptable creed, much difficulty was encountered. The general church possessed no creed. There were many statements of beliefs, used mainly in the sacrament of baptism, expressing in a manner which gradually had approached to uniformity the mind of the church respecting matters which had been brought into controversy. In the West, the short formula called the Apostles' Creed had gained wide acceptance. In the East, the local creeds tended to greater length. Eusebius of Cæsarea recited one which was in common use in his diocese. It seemed to the fathers to be both true and sufficient. Indeed, they were on the point of accepting it, when they perceived that it was equally acceptable to the Arians.

With such condition of happy agreement a conference in search of working unity would have been satisfied. Within the safe limits of such an inclusive formula they would have been content to leave conflicting details for future peaceful settlement, or even to have permitted a difference of opinion regarding matters which seemed so far beyond all human understanding. It was plain, however, to the Nicene fathers that the debate concerned the essential nature of the Christian religion. They saw in the doctrines of Arius a new invasion of old paganism. If Christ, as he said, was an inferior god, then Christianity recognized two gods; and if two, why not twenty? If the god Christ, why not the god Mithra? Why not the gods of Greece and Rome? Why not the endless æons of the Neoplatonists? Where was the line between Christianity and polytheism? And if polytheism were readmitted into theology, what power could keep it out of morals? The world was still pagan; the Christians were still in minority. The emperor, indeed, was on their side, but the emperor himself was almost as much a pagan as he was a Christian; he had not been baptized; in Rome he was still Pontifex Maximus, the official head of the old religion.

Under these conditions Arius came, a Christian polytheist. He came asking the recognition and approval of the church. The Nicene fathers saw behind him, waiting for the opening of the gates, all that pagan world with which they had contended, against which they had suffered martyrdom, over which they had for the moment triumphed. The pagan world, which had endeavored in vain to conquer the church by violence, was now endeavoring to conquer it by subtlety.

Thus when the creed which Eusebius offered was found to be so phrased that the Arians were willing to sing it, the fathers proceeded deliberately to insert into it a word which the Arians would not accept. This they found in the expression *homoousios*, which we translate by the phrase "of one substance." Jesus Christ, they said, is of one substance with the Father. The word was not contained in Holy Scripture. It had the further disadvantage of having been formally condemned and rejected in the discussion of the heresy of Paul of Samosata (268). But it met the necessities of the occasion. It expressed the mind of the orthodox, and no consistent Arian could pronounce it. The word was therefore written into the Eusebian formula, and the church was thus provided with a creed.

We believe in one God, Father Almighty, Maker of all things visible and invisible. And in one Lord, Jesus Christ, the son of God, begotten of His Father, only-begotten, that is of the substance (ousia) of the Father, God of God, and Light of Light, very God of very God, begotten not made, of one substance (homoousios) with the Father, by whom all things were made, both things in heaven and things on earth, who for us men and for our salvation, came down from heaven and was made flesh, and was made man, suffered, and rose again on the third day, went up into the heavens, and is to come again to judge the quick and the dead. And in the Holy Spirit.

This creed was signed. Arius and those who were loyal to his doctrine were excommunicated. The emperor added the sentence of exile. Several lesser matters were considered and decided. Then the council was adjourned. The bishops returned to their dioceses satisfied that the crisis was over, and that the great question was successfully and definitely settled.

III

The Wars of Theology

But the conference at Nicæa was like the conference at Jerusalem, which is reported in the Acts of the Apostles. The fathers and brethren at Jerusalem disposed, as they thought, of the difficulties involved in the relationship of Christianity to Judaism. They put Judaism out. They resolved that the Christian Church was an independent society, in no wise bound by the ceremonial laws which were written in the Bible. It was not necessary, they said, to keep the law of Moses in order to be a Christian. But the apparently unanimous decision of the conference was only the beginning of the debate. St. Paul, all his life long, was hindered and opposed by conservative Christian brethren who refused to accept the rulings of the Council of Jerusalem. The matter was too great and vital to be finally determined by any single assembly.

So it was with the Council of Nicæa. Even on the journey home, the fathers who had signed the creed began to be perplexed. Some of them were plain persons who felt that they had involved themselves in metaphysics beyond their understanding. It seemed to them that the simplicity of the gospel had been lost in the debate. Some of them objected to the Nicene Creed on the ground that it had introduced into religion a new and unproved word, of which the apostles had no knowledge. Some of them perceived on reflection that the difficulties which had been revealed by

115

Arius were real and serious, and were not satisfactorily settled by the taking of a vote. Certain influential bishops, such as Eusebius of Cæsarea and Eusebius of Nicomedia, had been on the side of Arius from the beginning, and had not been convinced by the action of the council. They had signed the creed, but with reservations. And these bishops were in a position to determine the opinion of the imperial court.

Moreover, in the air which all the Christians breathed was the spirit of paganism, with which Arianism was in subtle accord. Among the new Christians who had been attracted to the church, not by any deep conviction but by the imperial approval, there were many who had been nurtured in polytheism, to whom it seemed reasonable that there should be superior and inferior deities. It seemed to them that Arius, making Christ a lesser god, was reconciling Christianity with the doctrines of the philosophers, with the teachings of the ancient religions, and with the general wisdom of the world. Hardly, then, had the Nicene Creed been signed when the orthodox found themselves to their surprise, facing an Arian reaction.

In the long and bitter contention which ensued, the faith of Nicæa was defended and finally preserved by the courage and wisdom of Athanasius.

Athanasius was a native of Alexandria, where he had lived as a youth in the household of the bishop and had studied in the catechetical school. Before the meeting of the Council of Nicæa he had been ordained a deacon and had written a book on the Incarnation. When he accompanied Bishop Alexander to the council he was twenty-eight years of age. Soon after the adjournment of the council the bishop died, and Athanasius was chosen in his place. The city of Alexandria was at that time as preëminent in the East as Rome was in the West. Even the founding of Constantinople as a "New Rome" served rather to strengthen than to weaken the pride of the capital of Egypt. The bishops of the two cities contended for a supremacy which neither would yield to the other. Thus Athanasius was equipped for leadership by his high position, as well as by his strong conviction. At the same time the rivalry of the cities—Arian Constantinople against orthodox Alexandria—complicated the theological contention from the start.

The first campaign in the war of the theologians extended to the death of Constantine, in 337. The Nicene Creed remained formally in force, though many construed its articles so loosely as to defeat its purpose. Constantine would not permit any open attack upon it, but the bishops who were closest to him were friends of Arius. These Arian sympathizers and their followers busied themselves during the emperor's lifetime with attacks not upon the doctrine, but upon the administration of Athanasius.

The bishop of Alexandria held a difficult position. The clergy of the city could not forget the time when the bishop was not only elected but consecrated by themselves, and differed from them in office hardly more than a chairman differs from the members of a committee.[1] They asserted a traditional independence.

[1] Duchesne, *Early History of the Church*, I, 69; II, 99

One of them had disturbed the episcopate of Alexander by ordaining priests and deacons in his own right. They were now divided by the controversy which Arius had started.

Moreover, the Meletians were making trouble. Meletius, a bishop of Upper Egypt, had taken the austere side in the debate concerning the restoration of apostates, against the compassionate position of the bishop of Alexandria of his day, and had established schismatic parishes which called themselves the "Churches of the Martyrs." These churches vexed the soul of Athanasius, and he attacked them with the inconsiderate enthusiasm of youth. They complained of him to Constantine.

They said that Athanasius had sent emissaries to a Meletian priest named Ischyras, and that they had overthrown his altar and sacrilegiously broken his chalice. Athanasius was compelled to appear before Constantine and explain the matter. This he did by the testimony of witnesses who showed that messengers did indeed go from Athanasius, but that they found Ischyras ill in bed, so that any disturbance of a service was impossible.

Then they brought against the bishop the accusation of the Dead Hand. They said that he had murdered Arsenius, a Meletian bishop, and had cut off his right hand to use for the purposes of magic. Arsenius had certainly disappeared, and the accusers had the dead hand in their possession. To meet this charge, Athanasius was summoned to be tried by his brethren. The court sat at Tyre, in the church at whose consecra-

tion Eusebius had preached. The bishops who composed the council were of the Arian side. Athanasius
was confronted by his enemies. Standing there, however, to be tried for murder, Athanasius beckoned to a
veiled figure at the back of the church, and when this
mysterious person came forward and removed his veil,
behold the bishop Arsenius himself, not only alive, but
having his two hands! Even the most hostile could
hardly, under these circumstances, pronounce Athanasius guilty. They did, however, return to the charge of
the broken chalice, and on that charge and other accusations of violent action condemned and deposed him.

Immediately, Athanasius took ship and went to
Constantinople. He put himself in the way of the emperor and demanded a fair hearing. Thereupon the
bishops, who had now gone to Jerusalem to consecrate
the new church which Constantine, at the suggestion
of Helena his mother, had built over the Holy Sepul-
chre, withdrew the matter of the chalice and accused
Athanasius of threatening to hold back the corn fleet,
which carried the produce of the granaries of Egypt to
the markets of Constantinople. Then Constantine
perceiving in the midst of these perplexities that Athanasius had many enemies, and probably suspecting that
he had done something to deserve their hostility,
cleared his mind of the matter, and restored, as he
hoped, the peace of the church, by sending the accused bishop into banishment in Gaul.

During his residence in Gaul, Athanasius received word of the death of Arius. Arius had been
recalled from exile by the influence of his friends at
court, and had succeeded in convincing Constantine of

his sufficient orthodoxy. The emperor had ordered the aged bishop of Constantinople to receive the heretic on a certain day in the church, and to admit him to the Holy Communion. So important an event—whether it indicated the conversion or the triumph of Arius—was to be made an occasion of some festivity. The heretic was to go to the sacrament attended by a procession of his friends. But Arius was overtaken by a sudden hemorrhage, and his friends found him dead. Thus he passed out of the world into which he had introduced so much confusion, a man of eighty years, honest, devout, of stainless character, having the courage of his convictions, maintaining what he believed to be the truth in the face of the church which he believed to be mistaken, suffering hatred and exile and the loss of all things, that he might keep unbroken his loyalty to his reason and his conscience. We should remember him with respect; remembering at the same time that had his heresy prevailed the Christian religion—as Carlyle said—would have been degraded to a legend.

The death of Arius was followed by the death of Constantine. In his last hours the emperor put off his robe of imperial purple, and was attired in the white garments which were worn by those about to be baptized, and was admitted at last into the membership of the church over which he had so long presided as the bishop of the bishops. In Rome his monument was set among the statues of the divine emperors with the ceremonies of the old religion, but in Constantinople he was buried by the Christians, and about his tomb stood the twelve pillars which symbolized the twelve apostles.

The second campaign in the contention between the Athanasians and the Arians extended to the death of Constantine's son, the emperor Constantius, in 361. It was a time of theological discussion.

During this period no less than twelve councils of bishops were convened, until the pagans complained that the Christians had ruined the postal service by using the horses to convey them to the synods. Some of these meetings were held in the East, some in the West, some in the East and in the West at the same time, the different parties holding separate sessions. The East and the West took temperamentally characteristic positions: the speculative East eager to discuss the Nicene Creed and to amend it, the practical West content for the most part to take it as it stood.

Almost every council made its own creed. There appeared four creeds at Antioch, in the main orthodox but declining to use the test word *homoousios*. There appeared four creeds of Sirmium, departing farther and farther from the orthodoxy of Nicæa. The second creed of Sirmium was signed by Hosius, the veteran of the Nicene Council, now an aged and broken man. The creed of Ariminum (Rimini), dictated to the council by Arian leaders with whom the fathers conferred at Nice in Thrace, was signed by Liberius, bishop of Rome. "The whole world," said Jerome, "groaned, and was amazed to find itself Arian."

But Constantius failed to overcome Athanasius. At first he had recalled him from his banishment in Gaul, only to send him again into banishment in Rome. From Rome he was recalled, and the day of his return to Alexandria was long remembered as the festival "when the Pope Athanasius came home." The people thronged the streets to meet him with palm branches and fireworks. For five years he administered his diocese, and wrote letters and sermons and books in explanation and defence of the Nicene Creed.

Then finding that neither the imperial favor nor the imperial disfavor moved him, Constantius drove the bishop out of Alexandria with soldiers. He made his way into the Nitrian deserts, among the monks and hermits, where he spent six years in hiding. The world seemed to be against him, and he alone against the world. The state was Arian; the church was Arian. Everywhere the bishops were setting their signatures to Arian creeds. He was in the exceedingly difficult position of one who finds himself in disagreement with the church, and yet knows that the truth which he maintains is the truth of God. Shall he go out? Shall he say, "My understanding of the creed is disallowed by the majority of my brethren; on all sides the bishops are against me; I must resign my place"? Happily not. Athanasius believed that the church exists not for the maintenance of any position theological or ecclesiastical, but solely for the maintenance of the truth. Whatever is true, is of the essence of the church. Whatever is false, though it may be reiterated by endless councils, and confirmed by excommunication and anathema, is nevertheless nothing at all but heresy and schism and a lie, to be opposed by every honest man; to be opposed for the sake of the church as well as for the sake of the truth, and within the church.

The third campaign in the Arian war began with the accession of Julian and ended with the death of Valens.

Julian, abandoning the religion which seemed to him a hopeless tangle of controversy and endeavoring to restore the paganism of the great days of Rome, brought back all the exiled bishops, hoping that the Christians being left to fight their quarrels out with no restraint would so destroy the church that it would disappear like a bad dream. But when Julian's brief reign ended in defeat, it was the Arians in whom his hostile expectations were fulfilled. They were divided by the bitter discussions in the councils. All their initial differences were magnified. There appeared now not only Arians, but conservative Arians and radical Arians. Many who had been in sympathy with the Arian ideas were weary of the Arian debates. Many were scandalized by the spectacle of conventions of bishops set upon by Arian soldiers and compelled to sign their names to Arian creeds.

When Valens came to the throne he increased the confusion by taking the side of one Arian party against another. Thus they fought among themselves as Julian had devoutly hoped they would. In 378, when Valens fell at the battle of Adrianople, in his war against the Goths, Arianism as an organized party in the church came practically to an end.

By this time Athanasius had come to the end of his life of long contention, seeing victory and peace afar off, yet not entering himself into the new era. At the council held in Alexandria in 362, he made a notable contribution both to the theology and to the religion of the debating Christians. He discussed the words which were in use in the controversy and showed how a great part of the contention was due to a failure to define the terms. What we anti-Arians mean, he said, is this and this; and the more reasonable of his opponents found themselves in substantial agreement with him, after all. The result was the formation of a "New Nicene" party which was able to commend its theological position to the general Christian mind. The difficulty throughout had been the danger, on the one side, of a doctrine which recognized a superior god and one or two inferior gods, and, on the other side, of a doctrine which recognized in the "Son" and the "Holy Spirit" only names to distinguish functions or activities of God the Father. The church was in peril of shipwreck between the Scylla of Arianism and the Charybdis of Sabellianism. What they did under the leadership of Athanasius at the Council of Alexandria was to state the difference between *ousia* and *hypostasis:* *hypostasis* signifying a distinction of being, roughly and inadequately translated out of the Latin into English by the word *person; ousia* signifying a common essence or being, translated out of Latin into English by the word *substance.* We believe, they said, in one *ousia* and three *hypostases*, in one substance and three persons. This, said Gregory of Nazianzus, was more honorable and important and profitable than all the books which Athanasius wrote.

The Athanasian Creed is so called because of its expression of Athanasian orthodoxy. It was composed in the middle of the fifth century, probably in Lerins in

Gaul, and shows the influence of the theological teachings of Augustine.

CHAPTER VI

MONASTICISM IN THE EAST: BASIL AND GREGORY

I

The Beginnings of Monasticism

At the heart of monasticism is the vision of an ideal life. The true monk desires to get away from the temptation and distraction of the world, that he may dwell with God.

The belief that such a life could thus be realized was based on arguments derived from psychology and from philosophy.

The psychological reason for monasticism was drawn from the fact that the body affects the soul. Let us shut out all disquieting sounds and disturbing voices, and continue in silence, that we may have a composed spirit. Let us build a wall between us and the pride of the eye, that we may not see the splendor of the world nor be exposed to its solicitations. Especially, let us live in such a state that we may be free to discipline the body, to bring it into bondage that our soul may be at liberty, to minimize it for the magnifying of our spirit. It was discovered by primitive man that fasting induces a certain psychological condition, wherein, the body being abandoned and forgotten, the soul sees visions and hears voices, and attains the beatitude of ecstasy. It was found that protracted abstinence produced a gradual intoxication of the soul. It became one of the unsuspected luxuries of the saints.

The philosophical reason for monasticism was drawn from the theory that the body corrupts the soul. Matter being essentially evil, and the body being the source of all sin, our proper procedure is to make the body weak. Only by ascetic practices may we attain the victory of the spirit. The idea first appeared as heresy, being the doctrine of the Gnostics and of the Neoplatonists, but it took possession of the general mind. Especially in the East, it poisoned the souls of the saints. At its worst, it brought into being the mad monks—the grazing saints, who went about on their hands and knees and ate grass; the pillar saints, like Simeon Stylites; the chained saints, so fastened together that when one lay down to sleep the other was pulled up to pray. At its best, it made religion morbid, defying nature, contradicting the revelation of the will of God in the body of man, and glorifying hunger and thirst, and rags and celibacy and dirt, driving the saints into the deserts.

The tendency toward monasticism, psychological and philosophical, was assisted by the hardness and the badness of the world.

It was a hard world out of which men fled to save their lives. Some abandoned it on account of the cost of living. The burden of expense was made uncommonly heavy in the fourth century by a new method of financial administration in the empire. The patrician class, including many very rich men, was exempt from taxation. The slave class could not be taxed. Accordingly, all the responsibility for maintaining the government was put upon the plebeians, the men of business, merchants and manufacturers. They were compelled to serve in the curia of their town, and in that capacity had to pay the assessed taxes out of their own pockets. Thus they were at first impoverished and then ruined, and finally taxed out of existence. Some of them fled from the world. They sought the simple life of the monastery.

The heaviest hardship of the time was the continual tragedy of war. It was a universal curse. The contentions of the Christians among themselves, in riotous councils, in street fights, in pitched battles, continued until the defeat and death of the emperor Valens. And the victors at Adrianople were the barbarians, whose victory predicted the fall of the empire. These enemies occupied northern Europe and extended as far east as the boundaries of China. In the third century of our era, a tribe of them, the Huns, being defeated by the Chinese, were driven west. On their forced march they pushed against the Goths. The Goths, thus beset, gained permission from the Romans to cross the Danube, and settled in Thrace. There were more than a million of them. They became an intolerable menace. At last Valens attacked them, and was defeated, and the Roman army was ingloriously overwhelmed.

The Roman Empire received its death wound on that day. Thereafter, Goths, Huns and Vandals constantly beset the civilized frontier. They were like the Indians in the early days of American colonization. The annals of the time are filled with the sackings of cities, and with the murderous pillage of the countryside. Out of these troubles men sought safety in the monastic life. They made their way into remote and desert regions, into the wilderness, into the bleak mountains, to get out of the reach of these invading savages.

The world was not only hard but bad, and men went out of it to save their souls. One day, in Egypt, about the beginning of the last quarter of the third century (there is no definite record of either date or place) a young man named Antony, hearing in church the word of the Lord, "If thou wouldest be perfect, go, sell that thou hast, and give to the poor, and thou shalt have treasure in heaven: and come, follow me," obeyed. The three hundred acres which he had inherited from his father he divided among his neighbors, and betook himself to the desert. There he won those victories over divers temptations which Athanasius made famous in the book which he wrote about him. He was the first known pioneer of Christian monasticism.

Two contemporary witnesses, one pagan, the other Christian, testify to the prevailing wickedness of the world of the fourth century. The pagan witness is the honest historian Ammianus Marcellinus. He found the rich proud, selfish and cruel; he criticised their extravagance in dress, their enthusiastic racing and gambling, their excesses in eating and drinking. He found the poor pauperized and corrupted by state aid, fed at the public cost with corn, wine, oil and pork, and provided with free tickets to the plays and games which confirmed their brutality and lust. The Christian witness is St. Jerome. He describes society as tainted in every place with sensuality, a huge sin against the seventh commandment. These men were contemporaries in Rome in the fourth century. It is true that Ammianus was an old soldier, and that Jerome was an ascetic; and that they were thus inclined to judge their neighbors with severity. There is plenty of other evidence, however, that the nominal conversion of the Roman Empire to the Christian religion had effected no visible improvement in the common morals. The world was worse rather than better. Out of its besetting temptations men fled to save their souls.

They fled from the world, which in the first century was believed by the Christians to be doomed, and liable to be destroyed by divine fire before the end of the year, and which in the fourth century was believed by the Christians to be damned: it belonged to the devil. They fled also from the church, which they accused of secularity and of hypocrisy. Many of the monks were laymen, who in deep disgust had forsaken the services and sacraments. They said their own prayers and sought God in their own way, asking no aid from priests. They were men who had resolved never to go to church again.

Antony was a hermit rather than a monk. Finding a deserted fort on the bank of the Nile, opposite the Fayum, he made its walls a barrier between him and all mankind. He came not out, nor saw the face of man, for twenty years. But in the meantime others of like mind, fugitives like himself from the hardness and the badness of the world, had gathered about him. They had built their huts around his fort like the tents of a besieging army. They felt that to be near to him, even though they could not see him, was to be near to God in whose presence he lived. Thus the name "monk" (monos), which at first had meant one who lives alone, came to mean one who indeed lives alone but in company with many others also living alone in the same neighborhood. Antony found himself surrounded by a multitude of solitaries. At last he came out, in response to their calls, and taught them the rules which he had adopted for himself.

The next step was taken, a few years later, by Pachomius. In southern Egypt, near Dendera, he organized the monks among whom he lived into a community. Under his leadership their huts were arranged in rows, and the lane (laura) between them gave the name "laura" to this first monastery. He suggested a habit, a tunic of white sheepskin with a hood. Their prescribed food was bread and water, with a little fruit and vegetables, once a day. Pachomius appointed hours for prayer. Common meals and common prayers necessitated a refectory and a chapel. The life of the community was made more normal and healthful by the undertaking of regulated work: the brothers tilled the ground, and made mats and baskets which were sold for their support. Pachomius founded nine such monasteries for men and one for women, all under the same rule, and the number of these communities increased rapidly.

Thus beside the informal, partially regulated, Antonian monasticism of northern Egypt, grew this Pachomian monasticism of southern Egypt, in which the principle of solitude was displaced, in great measure, by the principle of brotherhood. The banks of the Nile and the adjacent deserts were populated by these devotees.

II

The Monks of Annesi

In the middle of the fourth century, at a time when there were no communities of monks outside of Egypt, two young men at the University of Athens determined to take up the monastic life. One was named Basil, the other was named Gregory.

Cappadocia, the district from which these two men came, had an unsavory reputation in the contemporary world. Cappadocia, Caria and Crete were called "the three bad K's" (tria kappa kakista). Men who had their residence in more favored regions liked to tell how a viper bit a Cappadocian, and the viper died. It was a forlorn land, they said, buried under snow in winter, and inhabited by timid and treacherous people. It lay to the south of Pontus, the country so maligned by Tertullian in his attack on Marcion. Nevertheless, Cappadocia had already produced an eminent saint in Apollonius of Tyana, the account of whose life was read by the Neoplatonists as the Christians read the Gospels. And the glimpses which we get of the homes of these youths are revelations of good Christian living.

Basil's grandfather and grandmother had suffered in the Diocletian persecution, and for seven years had lived in the wild woods of Pontus. His father, a man of wealth, was a famous teacher of rhetoric; his mother was celebrated for her beauty. Of their nine children,—four sons and five daughters,—three sons and three daughters were canonized as saints. The son who did not become a saint was a lawyer, and attained eminence as a judge; nothing is known of the unsainted daughters. Basil was at first taught at home by his father, and then sent to school in the Cappadocian Cæsarea. There he met Gregory.

Gregory's father was a bishop, whose diocese consisted of his own little town. He had once belonged to an obscure sect in which Christianity was mingled with Persian and Hebrew elements; fire was revered as the symbol of God, and the Sabbath was rigorously kept. There were many such bishops, each in his village church, like the early Congregational ministers of New England. And there were many such sects, little experiments in Christian eclecticism. Gregory's mother, however, was a person of such strictness of devotion, and so remote, from any idea of compromise, that she would not even look at a pagan temple when she passed it in the street. She took him to church, from the days of his earliest childhood, and dedicated him to the ministry. She did not, however, have him baptized: that was not yet the rule. Presently he was sent to study in Cæsarea.

The two friends went up to the University of Athens: first Gregory, then Basil. Years after, when Gregory preached the sermon at the funeral of Basil, he recalled their student days together, and told how he protected Basil from the customary initiation of freshmen. It was a rough ceremony which ended with the subjection of the novice to an involuntary bath. "I kept him from being hazed at college," said Gregory, "when he was a freshman."

Students gathered in great numbers, and from long distances, in the University of Athens. One of the contemporaries of Gregory and Basil was Julian, afterwards emperor and called the "Apostate." They studied rhetoric and philosophy: rhetoric meaning Greek literature,—the poets, tragedies and historians; philosophy meaning logic, ethics and physics.

Basil and Gregory were interested not only in rhetoric and in philosophy, but in religion. "Two ways were known to us, the first of greater value, the second of smaller consequence: the one leading to our sacred buildings and the teachers there, the other to secular instructors." They agreed that they would seek the monastic life together. Their studies ended, Gregory went home to help his father in his little diocese of Nazianzus; Basil undertook a journey to the East, partly for the joy of strange sights in strange lands, partly for the purpose of learning what manner of life the monks were living by the Nile.

In the course of his travels Basil visited the Antonian and the Pachomian communities. To his practical, administrative mind the life of brotherhood looked better than the life of solitude. This he resolved to practise. He returned to Cappadocia, full of enthusiasm, eager to recite the lessons he had learned, and called on Gregory to join him. After some debate as to the best place for a monastic retreat,—Basil preferring Annesi and Gregory preferring Tiberina,—they decided on Annesi. The decision was highly characteristic of the relationship between the friends: Basil was always temperamentally, and perhaps unconsciously, a domineering saint, with scant consideration for Gregory's opinions.

Annesi was a rocky glen, in Pontus, beside the river Iris. Basil described it in a letter. "There is a lofty mountain covered with thick woods, watered toward the north with cool and transparent streams. A plain lies beneath, enriched by the waters that are ever draining from it, and skirted by a spontaneous profusion of trees almost thick enough to be a fence; so as even to surpass Calypso's island, which Homer seems to have considered the most beautiful spot on the earth. Indeed, it is like an island, enclosed as it is on all sides; for deep hollows cut off the sides of it; the river, which has lately fallen down a precipice, runs all along the front, and is impassable as a wall; while the mountain, extending itself behind, and meeting the hollows in a crescent, stops up the path at its roots. There is but one pass, and I am master of it."

He was writing to Gregory, arguing for Annesi and making fun of muddy Tiberina. The breezes blow, he says, from the river, there are flowers and singing birds; and a deep pool is full of fish.

Gregory, speaking of the place after some experience of it, said that it was "shut in by mountains, so that the sun was rarely seen. The ground was encumbered by thorn-bushes, and was too precipitous for safe walking. The roar of the river drowned the voice of psalmody." He shuddered at the recollection of the biting winds, the cheerlessness of their hut, their fruitless labors in the so-called garden, and the poverty of their meals. Their teeth could make no impression on the solid hunks of bread. Thus Gregory, in his turn, made fun of the retreat preferred by Basil.

There they settled, where the summer verified the glowing praise of Basil, and the winter confirmed the laments of Gregory. No doubt, they encountered hardship: that is what they sought. Happily for their health, Basil's mother was living just across the river, and saw to it that the young monks did not starve. They said their prayers, and read the works of Origen from which they made a series of selections which they afterwards published. They went without food and without sleep, to their hearts' content. Other like-minded persons joined them. The ascetic spirit was in the common air of Cappadocia and Pontus. Already there were hermits, living as Antony had begun to live; and many others, keeping rules of strictness in their own homes. When a man like Basil, of wealth and high social station, a graduate of the University of Athens, betook himself to a glen beside a river, there were many to follow him. The conditions which had surrounded Antony and Pachomius surrounded him. And Basil and Gregory, like their predecessors in Egypt, were moved to make for themselves and their pious neighbors a rule of life.

Letters of Basil, and two series of Rules, preserve for us his ideals of the monastic manner of living.

In one letter, the second in a collection of more than three hundred, he discusses the matter in detail. We must strive, he says, after a quiet mind. He who lives in the world is exposed to perpetual distraction; he is anxious about his wife and children, worried by the care of his house and the oversight of his servants, distressed by misfortunes in trade and quarrels with his neighbors. Every day darkens the soul. The only escape is by the way of solitude. Let there be, then, such a place as ours, separate from intercourse with men, that the tenor of our exercises be not interrupted from without.

The day begins with prayers and hymns; thus we betake ourselves to our labors, seasoned with devotion. The study of the Bible is our instruction in our duty. This, too, is very important—to know how to converse, to be measured in speaking and hearing, to keep the middle tone of voice. As to dress, a tunic with a girdle is sufficient, avoiding bright colors and soft materials. Shoes should be cheap but serviceable. Beyond this, we pay no heed to our appearance. Indeed, garments not over clean and hair not smoothly brushed indicate a humble and submissive spirit. So, too, as to food: for a man in good health bread will suffice, and water will quench thirst; some vegetables may be added. Before and after eating, let grace be said. Let there be one fixed hour for taking food, that of all the twenty-four this alone may be spent upon the body. Let sleep be broken in upon by prayer and meditation.

Other details are added in a letter "On the Perfection of the Life of Solitaries." Basil advises silence. He speaks again of the modulated voice, and desires the seeker after God to avoid all rough and contemptuous answers, all wily glances and gestures of contempt. He advises poverty. He who comes to God ought to embrace poverty in all things.

Basil's "Longer and Shorter Rules," so called, are in the form of conferences or instructions. They appear to have been written by Basil with the help of Gregory for the communities which assembled around their retreat in Pontus.

They enjoin withdrawal from the world, and renunciation of all private property, though this is not enforced with thoroughgoing strictness. Hours are appointed for daily prayer: on waking from sleep, in the midst of the morning, at noon-day, in the midst of the afternoon, at the close of the day, on retiring to rest, at midnight, and before the dawn,—eight times. Watching and fasting are so regulated as to restrain excessive austerity; life is to be plain and simple, without needless distress. During meals a book is read, "and the brethren are to think more of what they hear than of what they eat." Bread and fish are appropriate, remembering the miracle in the wilderness. "To fast or watch more than the rest is self-will and vain-glory."

The Rules prescribe work as an essential part of life. Basil suggests the quiet trades, and such as do not minister to luxury,—weaving, shoe-making, carpentering, especially agriculture. The better educated among the brethren are to find their work in study, especially the study of the Bible; they are also to teach the young, who may be sent by their parents to the monastery school. The brethren are to engage in works of charity, ministering to the poor and caring for the sick, but in all cases for the sake of the soul rather than for the relief of the body.

Over the community is a superior, who assigns the tasks, and who is to be obeyed so long as his commands are not contrary to God's commandments. Other officers have their appropriate responsibilities. Confessions are to be made to the senior brethren, especially to those who are skilled in such ministration; the confessor exercises his office not because of appointment, but because of natural ability. Basil prefers many small communities, such as can have one lamp and one fire, as contrasted with the vast fraternities of Egypt. These communities he would have federated, with regular conferences of their superiors. Some communities will be of men, others of women,—the women making and mending the men's clothes; the men helping the women with their accounts, and administering the sacraments.

These Basilian Rules, which determined the ideals and the modes of life of monasticism not only in

Asia Minor but throughout the Eastern Church, and determine them to this day, improved upon the Antonian and the Pachomian Rules in their emphasis upon social duty. The disciples of Antony, in spite of their residence in a community, were at heart hermits; and although the monasteries of Pachomius brought the brethren nearer together, still the solitary life was regarded as more acceptable with God. But Basil organized a brotherhood. The monastic life, as he saw it, was to be lived in common. The dormitory, the refectory, the chapel, the work of the monastery farm, kept the monks together. Basil related them not only to each other, but to the outside world. He came to see that the best place for a monastery is not in the midst of a wilderness, but in the neighborhood of a city, where the school and the hospital of the cloister are accessible to the people.

Out of the serenity of this monastic life, Basil and Gregory were called into the active service of the church. Gregory went to help his father, the bishop of Nazianzus; Basil went to help the aged bishop of Cæsarea. In so doing they set an example which is still followed in the Eastern Church. In Greece, in Russia, to this day, the bishop is chosen from the monastery. It seemed at first to relate the church to the world. Out of the discipline of seclusion, in the strength of holy meditation, came the bishop, as the Master descended from the Hill of the Transfiguration to enter into social service in the plain. But the eventual result was to incapacitate the church for influential work. The bishops came from the monasteries ignorant of the world about them, speaking a language and living a life of their own. Before the fourth century was ended, the Eastern Church had retired from that control of public affairs into which the Western Church was triumphantly entering.

III

Basil, Archbishop of Caesarea

The world into which Basil and Gregory came was ruled by their old schoolmate Julian. He was attempting a restoration of paganism.

Julian had been brought up a Christian, but he hated Christianity. He despised the sophistries of his instructors, men of the Arian theology, who, neglecting the study of Christ and the gospel, occupied their time with the dreariest of metaphysical discussions. He turned to Homer and Hesiod, to Plato and Aristotle. He was repelled by the contentions of the Christians as they wrangled over points of doctrine, fighting in the streets and in the churches, debating theology with fists and clubs, and hating one another for the love of God. That secularization of religion, which was sending devout men out of the church into the monastic life, inclined Julian to seek for God in the old pagan way. It is a serious arraignment of the Christianity of the fourth century that Julian, earnest, pure-minded, sincerely religious, honestly devoted to the welfare of the empire, regarded it as he did.

It is at the same time an evidence of the substantial strength of the Christian Church that Julian was unable even to endanger it. He ordered the rebuilding of the temples which the Christians had destroyed, and the renewal of the sacrifices. He brought back deposed bishops whom his predecessors had exiled, leaders of heresies and schisms, and thereby increased the confusions and contentions of the church. He abolished the privileges which had been granted to the Christians, and forbade them to teach in the schools. He declined to interfere with the mobs who attacked the churches and the clergy. He brought the whole influence of his imperial power to the service of the pagan restoration. But it was like an endeavor to give life to the dead. The day of paganism had passed. It is said of Julian that he once asked, "What is the Galilean carpenter doing now?" and was answered, "He is making a coffin"—a coffin for dead paganism. It was believed among the Christians that when Julian died, in an inglorious war against the Persians, he cried, "O Galilean, thou hast conquered!" His endeavor to establish an imperial pagan church never even approached success.

After Julian came Valens. As Julian had attempted to make the empire pagan, Valens tried to make it Arian. This was a much more serious matter. The long controversy between the Arians and the Athanasians was in such a state that nobody could predict with reasonable confidence whether the faith of Nicæa, would be maintained or rejected. Athanasius was still living, but he was in the end of his days, and the next Pope of Alexandria was an Arian. The Pope of Constantinople was an Arian. Antioch was divided between two claimants of the episcopal office. The Pope of Rome was far away from the centre of the church, ignorant of the Greek language in which the debate was conducted and upon whose fine distinctions it depended, and much perplexed by the subtleties of the metaphysical discussion. There was crying need of a strong, clear-minded, influential orthodox leader, to come to the reinforcement of the losing side. He must be able to hold his own against a hundred bishops, and to withstand an emperor.

Such a man appeared in the person of Basil, now archbishop of Cæsarea. He took the direction of the cause of orthodoxy. His commanding personality, which had made him the founder of the new monasticism, made him the savior of the church. His energy was endless. He administered his vast diocese, preached persistently, fostered monasteries, established so great a hospital outside the walls of Cæsarea that it seemed a town by itself, wrote innumerable letters, published tracts and books which involved serious study, revised the liturgy, participated vigorously in a hundred controversies.

To him once appeared the Pretorian Prefect Modestus, sent by Valens to require him to conform to the Arian heresy or to resign. "Do you know," said the prefect to the prelate, "what I can do to you?"—"What can you do?"—"I can punish you with confiscation, with torture, and with death."—"Do your worst," said Basil. "All that I have is a few books and these clothes; you cannot exile me from the grace of God; and death will but bring me the sooner into His blessed presence."—"We bishops," he said, "are not arrogant, nor wantonly defiant; but where the cause of God is at stake, we despise all else: fire, sword, wild beasts, have no terror for us."

Presently, Valens came himself. Basil was in his cathedral, which was filled with a multitude of people. The responses in the service sounded like peals of thunder. The bishop stood, according to the ancient custom, behind the Holy Table, facing the congregation. His appearance—tall, with white beard, attired in the splendid vestments of his office—overawed the emperor. Valens had a conference with Basil, after which he sent him money for his hospital.

Meanwhile, Cappadocia had been divided into two provinces, and Cæsarea in Cappadocia Prima had a rival in Tyana in Cappadocia Secunda. The rivalry extended to the bishops. Each diocese depended for material support upon the produce of outlying farms; the servants of the two bishops fought at the crossroads. Thereupon Basil, after the manner of the big man whose overmastering strength makes him inconsiderate of his smaller neighbor, took his brother Gregory and set him down to hold the road at Nyssa, making him bishop of that place, paying no attention to his remonstrances. And he took Gregory his friend and put him down to hold the road at Sasima, making him bishop in the same way. Sasima consisted of a few houses around a posting-station. "There was no water, no vegetation, nothing but dust, and the never-ceasing noise of passing carts." Into these forlorn places Basil thrust the two Gregories, shy and gentle scholars. Thereby he lost their friendship for a time, though they forgave him. He set what he believed to be the good of the church above all friendships; only, in this instance, the good of the church consisted in the safe delivery of eggs and chickens from the Taurus Mountains. Gregory the brother remained at Nyssa; Gregory the friend, after a single look at Sasima, returned to Nazianzus.

In 378 came the battle of Adrianople, and Valens met his death. The Arian cause died with him. The next year Basil died, having seen only the beginning of that triumph of the Nicene faith to which he had so valiantly contributed. In the year following, Gregory of Nazianzus was called to Constantinople.

IV

Gregory, Archbishop of Constantinople

A new ruler had now established himself on the throne of the empire, the last ruler of the united Roman world. One night in Antioch, a little group of men of rank met in profound secrecy to ask a question of the Fates. The room had been purified by the burning of Arabian incense. In the middle of the floor was a great metal basin, having engraved upon its rim the letters of the Greek alphabet. In the basin stood a tripod made of laurel. Into the dim light of this darkened room came a sorcerer, in white, having in one hand a sprig of a tree, and in the other a thread of flax fastened to a ring. He seated himself upon the tripod, chanted an incantation to the gods who disclose the future, and swung the ring around the rim. The ring was thus to answer the question, Who shall be the next emperor of Rome? The magic ring touched first *Th*, then *e*, then *o*, then *d*. Thereupon the company in terror or in satisfaction stopped the sorcery, and fled each to his own house. But the secret was betrayed. Valens put some of the conspirators to death, and a number of good and innocent men whose names began with the fatal letters perished with them.

One of the victims of the fear and anger of the emperor was the great commander, Theodosius. He had been the ruler of Britain, where he had defended the Roman colony against the Picts and Scots. He had been the ruler of Africa, where he had quelled a dangerous insurrection. Upon the death of Theodosius, his son, of the same name, gave up his position in the army and retired to his farm in Spain. When Valens fell at Adrianople, Gratian, Emperor of the West, called Theodosius to be Emperor of the East.

Theodosius was still busy at the wars when Gregory appeared in Constantinople. It was not yet certain which side the new ruler would take in the controversy by which the church was divided. The city of Constantinople was almost wholly Arian. The orthodox congregation to which Gregory had come to minister was so weak and small that the services were held in a private house.

But Gregory was an unusual preacher. Lacking as he was in most of the physical advantages which assist public speech,—a short, slight, shy man, bald except for a thin fringe of gray hair, stoop-shouldered, and shabbily dressed,—he had a charm of voice, a directness of manner, an earnestness of purpose, and a divine gift of eloquence which profoundly impressed his hearers. He forgot his shyness when he arose to speak, and they forgot his looks. The house became a church, and the church was enlarged until its success alarmed the Arians. One night they stoned it.

The increasing congregation attracted the notice of an ecclesiastical adventurer, named Maximus. Gregory, simple-minded and unsuspecting, trusted him. But Maximus was the candidate of the bishop of Alexandria for the bishopric of Constantinople. If, as now seemed likely, the orthodox faith was to be restored in Constantinople, the bishop of Alexandria desired to secure the supremacy of his own see. So one night, a group of Egyptian bishops, having quietly arrived in Constantinople, and gained entrance by the key of a conspirator to Gregory's church, began the ceremony of consecrating Maximus. The proceedings were delayed by a curious incident. Maximus, who had thus far appeared as a Cynic philosopher, had not only the staff and the cloak but the long hair which belonged to that part. But the canons forbade the clergy to wear their hair long. It was therefore necessary, before the consecration could go on, to cut the flowing locks of Maximus. In the midst of this operation it was discovered that the philosopher's long hair was false. Then arose a tumult and disputing, in the course of which Gregory's congregation discovered what was happening in the church, and drove the Egyptians out with appropriate violence.

On a November day in 380, the emperor Theodosius arrived in Constantinople. He immediately decreed that the churches of the city should be taken from the heretics, in whose possession they had been for forty years, and restored to the orthodox. Two days later he himself escorted Gregory to the cathedral church of Santa Sophia. The sky was gray, and seemed uncertain whether to rain or shine. It was in keeping with the occasion. The orthodox faith had indeed come to its own again, but the procession in which Gregory walked beside the emperor had to be guarded by soldiers, while women wept and men cursed. The sun shone for a moment just as Gregory took his seat in the chancel, and the congregation shouted, "Gregory for bishop! Gregory for bishop!" But it was a sad triumph.

Theodosius called a conference of bishops, now numbered second in the list of the General Councils of the Church. They were, for the most part, from Syria and Asia Minor. The bishop of Alexandria came late, perhaps because he was invited late. The bishop of Rome seems not to have been invited at all. It was a local council. The bishop of Antioch, Meletius, presided; the contention there between Meletius and Paulinus had not been decided, but the party of Meletius was in the majority. Gregory was installed as bishop of Constantinople. Within a few days Meletius died, and Gregory was made president.

The council addressed itself to the discomfiture of heretics: Arians and semi-Arians, Sabellians, Marcellians, Photinians, Apollinarians, Eunomians, and Macedonians—a significant and portentous list. It endeavored to check the ambition of ecclesiastics, forbidding bishops to interfere with the affairs of dioceses other than their own, having special reference to the activities of Alexandria. The death of Meletius had revived the difficulty as to the episcopal succession in Antioch: the council tried to settle that.

It used to be thought that the Nicene Creed was phrased by this council in its present form, and to this is to be ascribed the inclusion of the conference among the General Councils; but there is no trace in the records of any discussion of this matter. The Nicene Creed, in its original wording, was that which had long been recited at Cæsarea, with the addition of certain Nicene words. The Nicene Creed, as it is said to-day, is that which had long been recited at Jerusalem. Cyril of Jerusalem, finding his orthodoxy questioned, may have presented this creed, with the proper Nicene additions, at the Council of Constantinople. Thus it may have come into general notice. It is interesting to find that after the long and tragic debate which had so seriously divided the church, the orthodox faith attained its abiding expression not as the result of any deliberation, and not with the sanction of any vote, but by the gradual commendation of its own merits.

The council debated with the fury of men who had faced each other on fields of battle. Gregory could not control them. He compared them to a flock of chattering jays, and to a swarm of stinging wasps. He wished to resign his presidency, but they would not consent. The bishop of Alexandria, however, when he arrived to add a new disorder to the scene, declared that Gregory having been made bishop of Sasima could not canonically be made bishop of Constantinople. Immediately, with a glad heart, he yielded up his presidency and his bishopric. He bade farewell to the council and the city, and returned to his Cappadocian farm. "I will rejoice," he said, "in my tranquillity, gladly flying from palaces, and cities, and priests." Once Theodosius invited him to attend another council, but he declined. "I will not sit," he said, "in the seat of synods, while geese and cranes confusedly wrangle."

In the shade of his trees, beside a singing brook, he wrote poetry and friendly letters. Sometimes he indulged himself for a while in the luxury of his old asceticism, sleeping on sackcloth, and once going a whole Lent without speaking. The wife and daughter of his kinsman Valentinian insisted on visiting him, till he likened them to Eve in the paradise of Eden: this was his chief annoyance. Thus he continued to the end of his gentle life, saying his prayers and tending his few sheep.

CHAPTER VII

AMBROSE

I

The Election of a Bishop

In the year 374, when the magician at Antioch was spelling out the name of Theodosius, a sudden crisis came in the life of a Roman governor named Ambrose. The father of Ambrose, as head of one of the departments of the empire, had ruled a great part of Europe. The son, at the age of thirty, was following in his father's steps. He was already set in authority over upper Italy. The chief city of his province was Milan. In 374, the people of Milan were assembled for the election of a bishop.

Episcopal elections had now become occasions of disorder. For example, Damasus, the contemporary bishop of Rome, the protector of St. Jerome and himself entitled "saint," had gained his place after an election so vigorously contested that when the enthusiastic debate was over, and the decision made, and the church emptied of the congregation, there were found upon the floor a hundred and thirty-seven bodies of dead electors.

This disorder was due in part to the secular importance of the office. The bishopric of a considerable city was a place of power and wealth. The bishop of a large diocese was the equal of nobles and princes, and did business with kings. The pagan prefect of Rome, Prætextatus, is reported to have said, "I will myself become a Christian, if you will make me bishop."

Another cause of disorder was the part taken in episcopal elections by the people. The choice of a bishop was a democratic undertaking. He might be selected at a town meeting. It is plain that a town meeting in Italy in the fourth century was very different both in tradition and in temperament from a town meeting of the present day in New England. The townsmen behaved themselves accordingly.

And the natural confusion and tumult of the occasion was frequently magnified, as in this instance in Milan, by bitter party strife. The long war between the Arians and the Athanasians was still an undecided conflict. Men went into the election of a bishop as if they were going into battle.

Thus the Christians assembled, under these critical and dangerous conditions, at Milan. The diocese was nearly as important as the see of Rome itself. Indeed, while that ancient city still shone in the light of the glory of its illustrious past, it had been politically superseded. The establishment of Constantinople, as a new Rome on the Bosphorus, and the division of the empire into two parts, East and West, had reduced the influence of Rome in the East to insignificance. Even the Western emperors had abandoned Rome, and had preferred to reside in Ravenna or in Milan. The city had ceased to be the centre of the world. When Chrysostom in his exile wrote to influential bishops in the West, protesting against the injustice of his condemnation, he addressed his letter in the same words to the bishop of Rome, the bishop of Milan, and the bishop of Aquileia, making no distinction.

Under these conditions, Ambrose came to the election to keep the peace. Standing at the bishop's throne, in the east end of the church, overlooking the crowded congregation, he addressed the people. Suddenly, in the midst of a moment's silence, a small child, lifted to his father's shoulder and seeing Ambrose in the bishop's place, called out in shrill surprise, "Ambrose is bishop!" Instantly the words were taken up, the rival candidates were forgotten, everybody shouted, "Ambrose is bishop!"

The possibility of such a position had never entered into the mind of Ambrose. The plans which he had made for his life were altogether different. A great noble, already well advanced in his civil career, he looked forward to political place and power. He was interested, indeed, in the Christian religion; he believed in it, and tried to live according to it; but he had not been baptized. Nevertheless, the people insisted, and Ambrose at last consented. Within the space of a single week he was baptized, confirmed, admitted to the Holy Communion, and made deacon and presbyter and bishop. Much of his property in land he gave to the church, much of his possessions in money he distributed among the poor. His business interests he entrusted to his brother.

He began the study of theology. Every day he celebrated the Holy Communion and preached. Every day he sat at a table in the hall of his house with his books before him, and the doors open. People came to consult him upon all manner of matters, great and small. In the free intervals between these consultations he gave his attention to reading, sometimes in the Bible, sometimes in the writings of Origen, sometimes in Plato. His mind was naturally conservative. He had an appreciation of the value of authority, which he had derived from his experience as a statesman. He desired to know the mind of the church, as expressed in the best traditions and in the instructions of the best teachers. This he would follow, this he would establish in his diocese. His inclination to accept and administer the doctrine and discipline of the church as he found it was confirmed by the conditions under which his ministry began. Absorbed immediately in the pressing business of his office, having no time for study except in the midst of his constant problems of administration, he was compelled to take things theological and ecclesiastical at the hands of tradition.

It was soon plain to Ambrose that his office in the church would bring him quite as close to the affairs of the great world as the office to which he had looked forward in the state. Milan being one of the capitals of the empire, and thus a place of residence for the imperial court, Ambrose had emperors and empresses among his parishioners. Into the responsibilities of this relationship he entered heartily.

Thus he was brought into two important contentions. He had his part in the last contest between Christianity and paganism, and in the last contest between orthodoxy and Arianism.

II

The Last Struggle of Paganism against Christianity

The Roman Empire had now been nominally Christian for more than half a century. But paganism continued. The persistence of the old religion in the country districts was so noticeable that the word "heathen," meaning one who lives on the heath, and the word "pagan," meaning one who lives in a village (pagus), bear witness to it to this day. The tillers of the soil were off the line of progress. The missionaries of Christianity addressed their message to the cities. Only very gradually did the new religion make its way into the back districts. On the hills and in the woods the gods were still worshipped in the old manner. Even in the cities, where there were many Christians, there were also many pagans. People do not put off one religion and put on another quickly. The beliefs which are involved are venerable, and the associations are too sacred, for that. Under the conditions of official change, while ancient institutions are established and disestablished, some citizens are instinctively hostile, some are friendly, some are enthusiastic, many are indifferent. The indifferent people are commonly in majority, going quietly about their accustomed affairs, letting their excited neighbors fight it out, paying to the combination of politics and religion no more attention than is absolutely necessary, and never consulting the morning paper before they say their prayers to see under what name God is to be addressed that day. Thus passive paganism continued into the Middle Ages. In the fourth century it was ready, upon any suitable occasion, to abolish the innovations of Christianity and to return to the old ways. Especially among the Roman aristocracy and in the Senate the men were many of them pagans; their wives and daughters might be Christians.

When the emperor Augustus returned from the battle of Actium, which made him master of the world, he set up in the Senate-house at Rome an altar dedicated to Victory, with a golden statue of that goddess standing on a globe in the attitude of forward flight. On this altar every senator for centuries had taken his oath of faithful service to the state. It was still the custom of the pagan members of that body to offer incense at this shrine. It represented the prosperity of Rome. In the general demolition of the images of the gods, the statue of Victory had escaped. It had been prudently covered when the emperor Constantius came to Rome. But the emperor Gratian had removed it. To this action he had been impelled by his Christian conscience, which also forbade him to wear the vestments of the pontifex maximus. It meant that the time of compromise had passed, and that the Christians who had pleaded in vain with pagan emperors for toleration intended to follow their intolerant example. When Valentinian II came to the imperial throne of the West a last attempt was made to secure to paganism the right at least to exist. A petition was presented to the emperor asking for the restoration of the altar of Victory.

The prefect Symmachus presented the petition, the bishop Ambrose presented the argument against it.

Symmachus declared that Rome with tears asked for the renewal of the ancient ceremonies. These rites, he said, had in the old time repulsed Hannibal, and driven away the invading barbarians. Ambrose remarked that the gods had been a long time in coming to the help of Rome against Hannibal; they had suffered nearly the whole country to be devastated. As for the barbarians, they had forced their way to the very walls of Rome, and would have entered had not the garrison been awakened by the cackling of frightened geese. "Where was your Jupiter that night?" asks Ambrose. "Rome has been saved in all her perils by the courage of her heroes."

Symmachus called attention to the fact that the removal of the altar had been followed by a famine, showing the displeasure of heaven. Yes, says Ambrose, there was a famine last year, but how about the unusual plenty of this year? Everybody knows that the years are different, that now there is abundance and now scarceness, in all lands and under all conditions of religion.

Symmachus pleaded for the ancestral ways. But life, says Ambrose, consists in progress. The world has grown since the beginning of creation; we ourselves grow year by year. Can we maintain, then, that infancy is better than maturity? Shall we say "that all things ought to have remained in their first beginnings, that the earth which was at first covered with darkness is now displeasing because it is brightened with the shining of the sun?"

The arguments of Ambrose were effective with Valentinian; who, indeed, needed no arguments, his mind being already made up against the restoration of the altar. They are interesting as showing how far Christianity had come on in the Roman world since the apologies of Justin Martyr.

The attempt of paganism to save itself by the peaceful method of petition having thus failed, an attempt was made to preserve the old religion by wager of battle.

Valentinian II being but a youth, Theodosius had given him as prime minister, and practical administrator of imperial affairs, Arbogast the Frank. The appointment discloses the gradual manner in which the barbarians were effecting the conquest of the empire. Sometimes, indeed, they proceeded by invasion, but often they came quietly, by dint of individual ability, into places of power. Then being in place, and possessing the power, they used their opportunity. One day, Valentinian, irritated beyond endurance, discharged Arbogast. The prime minister brought the letter of dismissal into the presence of the emperor, tore it in pieces before his eyes, and said, "You are not my master." A few days later Valentinian was found strangled, and his throne was given by Arbogast to a schoolmaster, Eugenius, a teacher of grammar.

The new government sought to reinforce itself against the inevitable vengeance of Theodosius by calling to its side the forces of the old religion. The altar of Victory was replaced in the Senate-house, the closed temples were reopened, the abandoned and forbidden ceremonies were resumed. As the pagans marched to meet Theodosius among the foothills of the Alps, they vowed that on their victorious return they would stable their horses in the cathedral of Milan. The armies met beside the river Frigidus, north of Trieste, as Constantine and Maxentius, fifty years before, had met in the same kind of contention, between Christianity and paganism, beside the Tiber. At first the armies of the pagans prevailed. Then Theodosius prayed, as Constantine had prayed before. He led his army into battle crying, "Where is the God of Theodosius?" A great storm arose, the snow was blown fiercely into the faces of the foe. It was as when the stars in their courses fought against Sisera. And the Christians won.

Thus finally fell the ban of the empire on the ancient paganism. It lingered long in secret places, in recesses of the woods and hills. Here and there it rose, now and again, in local, ineffectual protest. Gradually it got itself baptized with the names of Christian saints. Thus far it is alive to-day. But with the denial of the petition of Symmachus and the defeat of the forces of Eugenius and Arbogast its existence as a recognized religion came to an end. The sons of Arbogast and Eugenius sought refuge in Milan with Ambrose, and by his intercession their lives were spared. The fact is a symbol of Christianity as a friendly conqueror, at war with paganism but not with pagans, seeking not captives but converts.

III

The Last Struggles of Arianism against Orthodoxy

While the Christians were thus contending with the pagans, another war was coming to an end, the war of the orthodox against the heretics.

The Nicene faith was now, indeed, the established creed of the empire. But Arianism continued. The intellectual difficulties which had brought it into being were not sufficiently met by the imposition of a theological formula. Theodosius had attempted to stamp out Arianism by a series of decrees against it, but the enactment and reenactment of the same decrees show that it had not been found possible, or expedient, to enforce them.

The Theodosian laws ran with much more difficulty in the West than in the East; for the empress Justina, widow of Valentinian, and mother of the young emperors, Gratian and Valentinian II, was an Arian. There ensued accordingly between Ambrose and Justina a strife similar to that which Chrysostom waged with Eudoxia. The conditions were different, in that the contention in Constantinople turned upon matters social and moral, while the contention in Milan turned upon matters theological. The results also were different, because the representative of the church in the one case had been trained in monastic life, apart from the world, while the representative of the church in the other case had been trained in political life, coming to his ministry straight from the governorship of a province.

Twice Justina had appealed for aid to Ambrose. Twice Ambrose had gone at her request to meet the usurper Maximus. Maximus had taken advantage of the imperial situation in the West. The death of the emperor Valentinian had left Justina with her two sons, Gratian aged seventeen, and Valentinian II aged four. The usurper had come down with the legions of Britain at his back, had defeated and killed Gratian, and had taken into his possession the lands of Gaul and Spain. In a first conference Ambrose had held him back from Italy until the passes were secured. A second conference, however, had been unsuccessful. Down came Maximus over the Alps, and Theodosius had to come and meet him in battle. When the weakness of Maximus became evident, his own soldiers seized him, tore his robe of purple from his back and his sandals from his feet, and dragged him bound into the presence of Theodosius.

The part thus taken by Ambrose in these public perils indicates not only his political wisdom and his commanding personality, but the importance of his office. He speaks and acts as a bishop on behalf of his people. As citizens, indeed, they belong to the civil authority, to Justina; but as Christians they belong to the ecclesiastical authority, to Ambrose. The inevitable contention between these two authorities arose by reason of the request of Justina that a church in Milan might be used by the Arians.

There were many Arians in Milan. The bishop who had preceded Ambrose was of that belief. The court was largely Arian. The Goths who composed the imperial garrison were Arians.

These Gothic soldiers were disciples of a missionary bishop whose great place in the life of the fourth century, and in the progress of religion and of civilization, has been obscured by the fact that he labored among the barbarians, and that the Christianity which he taught was of the Arian kind. Neither Basil nor Gregory nor Chrysostom nor Ambrose exerted an influence so determining and important as did Ulfilas, the Apostle to the Goths.

The parents of Ulfilas had been carried captive out of Cappadocia in one of those incursions of the third century when the Goths destroyed the temple of Diana at Ephesus, and spared the library at Athens, in order, as they said, that the Greeks might be encouraged to read and not to fight. The lad had grown up among the Goths, and had come to understand them as if they were his brothers. His parents taught him Greek and Latin, and in the ten years he spent as a hostage, or an envoy, in Constantinople, he learned theology. The city was then Arian, and he took Christianity as he found it there. He was made a missionary bishop, and returned to the Goths, among whom he labored to the end of his days. A chief source of information about him is an account of his life written by a pupil of his, Auxentius, whom Ambrose succeeded in the bishopric of Milan.

Ulfilas made two inestimable contributions to the history of Europe: he translated the Bible into the Gothic language, and he converted the Goths. Ulfilas found the Gothic language spoken but not written. The Goths and their Teutonic neighbors, the eventual conquerors of the empire and the progenitors of modern Europe, had no literature. Ulfilas invented an alphabet out of Greek and Latin and Runic materials, and thereby, translating the Bible, produced the first book in that language which was the mother of German and of English. The words and sentences of Ulfilas differ from the words and sentences of Luther as the English which is spoken at the age of eighteen months differs from the English which is spoken at the age of eighteen years. The name of Ulfilas stands thus at the beginning of all Teutonic writing. He was the father of it.

At the same time, as the "Moses of the Goths," he had his great part in that conversion of the barbarians which preserved the church in the midst of the downfall of the empire. Had it not been for him, the invaders might have dealt with the church in the West as the Moslems dealt with the church in the East. The soldiers of Justina's bodyguard, Goths but yet Christians, represent the mission of Ulfilas. There is a tradition that he omitted from his translation the books of Samuel and Kings because there was so much fighting in them. He was afraid that his Goths would like these books better than the Gospels. The age was filled with the tragedy of war, but it would have been worse had it not been for the ministry of Ulfilas.

Under the decrees of Theodosius, the Arians, whether they were soldiers or courtiers, had no church in Milan. Their places of worship had been taken from them. Justina asked that they might have a church, either the Portian Basilica outside the walls, or the New Basilica within. The request seems a reasonable one. "An emperor," said Justina, "took our churches away, now an empress would restore one of them."

Ambrose dealt with the matter as he dealt afterwards with the demand of Theodosius, that the Christians rebuild a synagogue which they had burned. He said that the rebuilding of a synagogue was against religion. He declined to consider the justice of the case. He intimated that the Jews may have burned their own synagogue so that the Christians might be compelled to build them a better one. Anyway, he said, it was a cheap synagogue; the whole town of mean houses was of little value. And remember, he added, how the Jews used to burn our churches: we never got anything back from them. But the main point is that we are right and the Jews are wrong, and that in a contention between such sides justice does not count. This, said Ambrose, has to do with religion; concerning pecuniary causes consult your officers, but concerning religion consult the priests of God.

He took the same course with Justina. It is impossible for us, he said, to surrender a church in which you may worship according to the errors of heresy. In a letter to his sister, Ambrose described the contest which ensued. "Some great men," he says, "counsellors of state, begged of me to give up the basilica, and to manage that the people should make no disturbance. I replied, of course, that the temple of God could not be surrendered by a bishop." The next day was Palm Sunday, and it was reported to Ambrose in the New Basilica that men were putting up the imperial hangings on the outer walls of the Portian Basilica to mark it as the property of the court, and that the people had seized an Arian priest and were at that moment beating him in the street. Ambrose sent and rescued the man from further violence. At the beginning of Holy Week, fines were laid upon the merchants of Milan for their sympathy with Ambrose, and preparations were made to have the doors of the Portian Church forced by the soldiers, and the defenders who were within thrown out. Again the counts and tribunes begged Ambrose for the sake of peace to yield to the imperial demand. They feared the raising of a tumult which might destroy the city. But Ambrose would not yield. Indeed, it became so plain that he had the people on his side that none of the Arians dared appear alone upon the streets.

The services of the Holy Week proceeded, and Ambrose preached daily upon the appointed lessons from the Book of Job. He commented upon the statement that Job's wife urged him to curse God and die. He referred to other women in the Bible who had been in error: Eve, he said, deceived Adam, Jezebel persecuted Elijah, Herodias procured the death of John. He did not apply these illustrations to the conduct of Justina. He left the congregation to do that. As the week went on the state of public opinion was so plain that some of the hangings on the Portian Church were cut down by the boys. Even the soldiers sided with the bishop. At last, on Good Friday, the court withdrew the soldiers, repaid to the merchants the fines which had been imposed upon them, and confessed defeat. Ambrose told his sister that when the nobles were entreating the young emperor to yield he said, "If Ambrose bade you, you would deliver me up to him in chains."

A year passed, and the struggle was renewed. By this time the Arians had elected a bishop of their own, another Auxentius. Under his influence Valentinian issued a decree which was understood to give liberty of worship to Arians, and to put the orthodox in peril. It sounded like the renewal of the war of religion, and the revival of persecution. Ambrose refused to enter into a public debate with Auxentius. There was nothing, he said, in his position which he could change; there was no room for concession or for arbitration. It was rumored that his life was in danger.

Ambrose took up his residence in the New Basilica, and the people continued with him to defend him, day and night. Finding that the time was likely to be long, and perceiving the need of keeping up the courage of his devout garrison, he introduced into the services in which they were continually engaged that antiphonal manner of singing which Chrysostom undertook to use against the Arians in Constantinople.

To this singing Ambrose contributed both words and music. He took the ancient melodies of

Christian worship,—derived perhaps from the synagogue, or perhaps from the cadences of the chorus in
the Greek plays, or perhaps from the natural intona-
tions of the voice,—and set them in definite order,
making the kind of chant which is called "plain-song."
Afterwards Gregory developed the Ambrosian chant
into the Gregorian.

Ambrose wrote hymns, some of which continued long in the worship of the Western Church.
Augustine says that Monica, his mother, attended these
meetings, and he records the impression made on his
own soul by the music which Ambrose had thus enriched. "How did I weep," he says, "in thy hymns and
canticles, touched to the quick by the voices of thy
sweet-attuned church! The voices flowed into mine
ears, and the truth distilled into my heart, whence the
affections of my devotions overflowed, and tears ran
down, and happy was I therein."

From his retreat in the New Basilica,—already
called the Church of Ambrose and retaining that title
to this day,—the bishop defied his enemies. Against
Auxentius the Arian, he preached with all confidence.
"I see," he says to the congregation, "that you are
unusually excited and disturbed to-day, and that you
are watching me with all your eyes. I wonder why.
Have you heard that I have received an imperial order
from the tribunes that I may depart in peace, provided
only that I leave the city? To that order I returned the
reply that the wish to desert the church has never
entered into my mind. I fear the Lord of the universe,
but I do not fear any emperor on earth." "The emperor," he added, in words which served as texts for

sermons for a thousand years, "the emperor is within the church, not above it." "As for the soldiers, the clash of whose arms you hear as I speak, do not be afraid of them; they will not harm you."

In the midst of this state of siege there appeared unexpected reinforcements. Ambrose describes the dramatic event in one of his letters to his sister. The people asked him, he says, to consecrate the church, and especially to hallow it, if possible, with relics of martyrs. He replied that he would do so if he could find any. Then, he says, "a kind of prophetic ardor seemed to enter my heart." Under the influence of this "ardor," he sent men to dig away the earth before the chancel screen of the Church of St. Felix and St. Nabor. And as they dug, behold, the blood and bones of two men of marvellous stature! Surely, cried the oldest inhabitants, the bodies of Protasius and Gervasius, martyrs long forgotten! To this happy identification the relics immediately and generously responded. A blind man, named Severus, who had been a butcher but had lost his job by reason of his failing sight,—the details are from Ambrose's letter,—did but touch the hem of the cloth which covered these precious relics when his eyes were opened, and he saw plain; and others who followed him were likewise healed.

The martyrs were brought over to the Ambrosian Basilica and buried beneath the high altar. There stand their tombs in the crypt to this day. The two saints had come to the rescue of the true faith as the two gods, Castor and Pollux, came to the aid of the Romans at Lake Regillus. The new enthusiasm swept the city, it was now so clear, beyond all doubt, that

Heaven was on the side of Ambrose, that the Arian aggression ceased.

IV

The Penitence of Theodosius

The most dramatic event in the life of Ambrose, exceeding his debate with Symmachus over the altar of Victory, and his contention with Justina over the possession of the churches, was his repulse of Theodosius after that emperor's great sin.

Theodosius, both in position and in person, was one of the greatest of the emperors of Rome. He was the last ruler of the undivided empire, the last sovereign to bear sway both in Constantinople and in Rome. But he was an unsuccessful ruler of himself. Upon a memorable and tragic occasion he lost his self-control over the conduct of the people of Thessalonica. On the eve of a chariot-race in which the Thessalonians were excitedly interested, one of the chief charioteers committed an abominable crime, and the governor, Botheric, put him in prison, and refused to let him out, even for the race. Thereupon the city rose in riot, released the prisoner, and put the governor to death. Theodosius, urged by his ministers of state and by his own fierce anger, sent a company of soldiers to take vengeance on the city. One account says that the people were assembled in the circus, and that the soldiers, marching in and locking the gates behind them, killed everybody in sight. Accounts agree that the massacre lasted for three hours, and resulted in the murder of seven thousand persons. The innocent perished with the guilty.

The tragedy stirred even that blood-stained world. It was perceived to be a crime not only against religion, but against civilization. It was an assertion that the sovereign is outside the range of law and justice, and may work his own will without restraint. That was a commonplace with Caligula and Commodus, but the world was older now and the emperor was supposed to be a Christian, "within the church," as Ambrose said, "not above it": within and not above the kingdom of Christ.

Ambrose wrote to Theodosius. "Listen, august Emperor," he says. "I cannot deny that you have a zeal for the faith; I do confess that you have the fear of God. Nevertheless, there was that done in the city of the Thessalonians of which no similar record exists in the history of the world. Are you ashamed, O Emperor, to do that which royal David did, who when his offence was pointed out, and he was condemned by the prophet, said, 'I have sinned against the Lord'? Put away now this sin from your kingdom: humble your soul before God. Sin is not done away but by tears and penitence. I am writing with my own hand that which you alone may read. I had a dream about you, that you came to church, and that the Lord did not permit me to offer the holy sacrifice while you were present. The dream was a revelation of the truth. You are to pray, you are to repent; then, and not till then, may you approach the table of the Lord."

The Church of St. Ambrose in Milan is still approached by a cloistered courtyard, opening from the street. The present structure is perhaps no earlier than the twelfth century, but the courtyard follows the ancient lines, and the oak door, carved with scenes from the life of David, is said to have belonged to the original church. There Ambrose met Theodosius. The emperor, paying no attention to the letter, was about to enter when the bishop repelled him. He laid hold upon Theodosius by his purple robe, and turned him away.

It is one of the supreme scenes of history. We remember as we look upon it how Henry IV of Germany stood barefoot in the snow at Canossa before the closed door of Pope Gregory VII, and how Henry II of England suffered himself to be scourged by the monks of Canterbury for the death of Thomas à Becket. It was a precedent for ambitious prelates throughout the Middle Ages. Here the church confronted the state, and rebuked the ruler of the world.

But of all this there was no more in the soul of Ambrose than in the soul of Nathan before David, or of John the Baptist before Herod. Ambrose had, indeed, the pride of his order. It is true that he once said that priests ought to judge laymen, and not laymen priests. It cannot be denied that he behaved himself as an ecclesiastic rather than as a Christian in the matter of the rebuilding of the synagogue. He was an imperious person temperamentally and officially. But that day at the church gate he represented the Christian ideal of a right life over against the spirit of the world. The church, speaking by his voice, was at its best that day.

Theodosius was the greatest man on earth, the ruler of the world, but Ambrose was stronger than Theodosius in the strength of the moral law of God.

Eight months passed before the emperor was readmitted to the church. They liked to tell in the old days, how he laid aside his imperial robes and spent the time in prayer and penitence, and how, coming at last a humble suppliant and received by Ambrose, he prostrated himself upon the floor of the church in the presence of the congregation, crying with tears, "My soul cleaveth unto the dust; quicken thou me according to thy word." It is certain that Ambrose subjected Theodosius to penitential discipline, and that he required him to make a law, which is still in force in Christian countries, that a space of thirty days must intervene between condemnation and punishment.

One day, after the emperor had been restored to the privilege of the Holy Communion, he remained in the chancel among the presbyters. Remembering how his predecessor Constantine had been the head of the church, and the bishop of the bishops, even before he was baptized, such a place of honor seemed appropriate. The kings of the old order, David and Solomon and their successors, had offered the sacrifices: were not the kings of the new order as good as they? The polite Nectarius, who preceded Chrysostom in the bishopric of Constantinople, formally invited Theodosius to a place in the sanctuary. Not so Ambrose. He sent a messenger to remind the emperor that "the purple makes emperors, not priests." And Theodosius quietly took his place among the laymen.

It meant at the moment that the man with the gold ring was being treated according to the counsel given in the Epistle of St. James. Ambrose had no respect of persons. It meant also that there was a spiritual power in the world before which the claims of wealth and position had no place. The time came when imitators of Ambrose were filled with ambition, and authority in the chancel was no more spiritual or moral than authority in the nave: they were both secular together, differing only in their dress. But in the time of Ambrose, and long after, the great need of the confused and troubled world was a clear assertion, such as he made, of the ever-lasting supremacy of religion.

In the beginning of his *Life of Ambrose*, Paulinus, who had been his secretary, says that in his infancy as he lay asleep in his cradle a swarm of bees settled on his face; and that in his old age, as he preached, a flame of soft fire glowed about his head. It is remembered of him that he was as kind as he was commanding. One time, to pay the ransom of captives taken in battle, he took the silver vessels from the altar, melted them down and sold them. He was a plain, uncompromising, faithful and fearless preacher. "When I came down from the pulpit," he wrote to his sister, "the Emperor said, 'You spoke about me.' I replied, 'I dealt with matters intended for your benefit.' "

CHAPTER VIII

CHRYSOSTOM

The ministry of John, who for his eloquence was called Chrysostom, the Golden Mouth, falls into four divisions. It begins with his austerities as a monk in the mountains of Syria, and ends with his banishment and death among the mountains of Armenia; between this prologue and this epilogue are the twelve years of his activity as a preacher in Antioch and the six years of his activity as a bishop in Constantinople.

I

The Pagan River and the Christian Mountain

The city of Antioch lay between a pagan river and a Christian mountain.

The river was made pagan by the Grove of Daphne, a pleasure-garden on its bank. The garden was ten miles in circumference, planted with laurel and myrtle, with cypress trees and scented shrubs, and watered by running streams. In the midst stood a noble temple dedicated to Apollo, and commemorating the legend that in this place Daphne, pursued by the wanton god, had been transformed into a laurel tree. The temple was built of polished marble and carved cypress, and contained an image of Apollo, blazing with gems.

The emperor Julian, coming to consult the oracle, had found it dumb, and after repeated efforts to gain a reply had been informed that the god was silent because the place was polluted by the presence of a dead body. These words pointed plainly to the relics of the Christian martyr Babylas, whose chapel stood beside the temple, and whose fame at that time exceeded the sanctity of Ignatius, and even of Paul and Peter. Julian ordered the removal of Babylas and the order was obeyed, but the translation was effected with a long procession and a splendid ceremony whereby the Christians, while yielding to the emperor, defied him. That night the temple of Apollo—perhaps struck by lightning, or perhaps not—was burned to the ground.

One of the boys who joined in the procession and went to see the fire was the John whom we know as Chrysostom. In this he was encouraged by his devout mother, Anthusa. She had been left a widow at the age of twenty, having this only child now fifteen years of age. She had brought up her son in the Christian faith.

The lad came under the influence of two effective teachers. One was the pagan Libanius, master of rhetoric, who said afterwards that Chrysostom should have been his successor if the Christians had not stolen him. The other was the Christian Diodorus, whose "pale face, sunken cheeks and emaciated frame" had aroused the ridicule of Julian, who accounted it absurd that God could care for a man of his mean appearance. Libanius made John an orator; Diodorus made him a saint.

Diodorus was the abbot of a monastery in the mountain which was made Christian by its use as a sanctuary. The woods which covered the slopes of the hills were filled with monks, some solitary, some in companies, fasting and praying. The heart of Chrysostom turned toward the mountain. Every day he lifted up his eyes unto the hills, turning his back upon the river. Antioch was so corrupt a city that Latin moralists declared that it poisoned even the air of Rome. It was as beautiful as it was wicked. It made vice attractive. But its temptations did not allure Chrysostom. He was intent with all his heart upon the life of the spirit. At first he lived at home, obeying the wish of his mother, making his room a monastic cell. Then he sought the nearer presence of God on the heights of Mt. Silpius. For a time he lived in community, practising asceticism moderately; then he became a hermit, practising asceticism beyond the boundaries of reason. He tried to live as if he had no body.

After four years of this experience Chrysostom came down from the mountain, having strengthened and enriched his soul with prayer and meditation, having filled his mind and his memory with the words of the Bible, but having seriously impaired his health. He had cultivated his spirit, but had ruined his digestion.

II

At Antioch

Returning to Antioch, he was ordained, and entered into the active work of the ministry. He began to preach. Coming out of the solitude of the woods, from those years of silence, and now appearing among men, like John the Baptist, he attracted immediate attention. He took what old Libanius had taught him and used it in the service of religion. To the art of the orator which he had learned he added the spirit of a prophet. He became in Antioch what Demosthenes had been in Athens, and Cicero in Rome.

In this he had no help from a commanding presence. He was a small, slender, bald man, without even the assistance of a strong voice. But what he said was clear and definite, nobody could mistake what he meant; he had emotion, he had humor, he had sympathy, he had passion, he had the exuberant style which his Syrian congregation liked. And he addressed himself straight to common life. In the midst of the inveterate dissensions of the church of Antioch, where the Christians who should have cleaned the town were debating matters ecclesiastical in the temper of hostile partisans, and matters theological which were as remote from the needs of Antioch as lectures on the political opinions of the citizens of the moon, Chrysostom was neither theologian nor ecclesiastic. He was profoundly concerned about practical morality, the enemy of moral evil and the advocate of righteousness. That which was of supreme importance to him—for the sake of which both creed and church existed—was character.

The sermons of Chrysostom were taken down in shorthand, and we have them as he spoke them. He stood on a platform in the midst of the church, where he could touch his nearest listeners with his hand. The word "homily" describes these discourses in their informality and familiarity. He was accustomed to take his text out of the Bible in order, verse by verse, and chapter by chapter. Thus he expounded the Scriptures. For example, he preached ninety sermons on the Sermon on the Mount. In the course of his ministry he went thus over almost the entire Bible. The sermon began with the text, and then proceeded freely now in this direction, now in that, as the preacher's mind invited him, ending always with a practical application. There was rarely any single theme, rarely any process of argument, never a logical succession of points such as appeared in the discourses of the preachers of the Reformation and of the Puritan Revolution. Chrysostom was as discursive as a honey-bee, in whose wanderings there is no consistency, except the consistent purpose to go wherever there is honey, and to get as much of it as possible. Meanwhile the congregation, when the preacher pleased them, freely applauded.

Chrysostom censured the social follies of the people. He criticised with much plainness of speech the attire of the women. He was as concrete as Isaiah. He objected to their false hair and their painted faces, to their cloth of gold, their perfumes and their necklaces, their mules splendidly harnessed, their black servants adorned with silver, and to the idle and selfish lives of which these were the symbols. With equal plainness he told the men that they ate too much and drank too much, and were overfond of plays and games. "Answer me," he said, "what do you talk about? About dinner? Why, that is a subject for cooks. Of money? Nay, that is a theme for hucksters and merchants. Of buildings? That belongs to carpenters and builders. Of land? That is talk for husbandmen. But for us, there is no other proper business save this, how we may make wealth for the soul." He objected to their banquets, and not to those only which were held in the houses of the rich. "This advice," he says, "I am giving not to the rich only, but to the poor too, especially those that club together for social parties, with shouts and cheers and low songs, followed by headaches." He was of the opinion of Aristotle who said that "general discourses on moral matters are pretty nearly useless"; it is in particulars that effective truth is told.

The preacher addressed himself to the everlasting problem of poverty and riches. He dealt with the slavery of the time, endeavoring not to remove but to mitigate it. How often, he said, as I pass your houses in the street, I hear the mistress screaming in fury, and the maid crying in pain. He told the rich that they made their employees work like mules, and cared no more for them than for the stones in the pavement. Empty-handed, he said, and in debt they return from their hard labor. He rebuked the vice of avarice. All evil comes from "mine" and "thine." Fortunes are made by injustice, by violence, by dishonesty, by monopoly, by taking interest at twelve per cent.

The preacher complained, with a frankness which many a discreet parson of our own day may envy, of the absence of the people from the services of the church. No discomfort, he says, no stress of weather, will keep you from the circus, while a cloud the size of a man's hand will keep you from the service. He complained of the behavior of the congregation. Prayer is going on, and all are kneeling, but not all are praying; some are stupidly unconcerned, some are talking, some are laughing. It is impossible for me, he says, to see all that is going on, but you see it. Why do you not put a stop to it? If you were at home and saw a silver plate tossed out of doors, you would go and pick it up. Help me, in like manner, to keep devout order in the church. People act in the house of God as if they were in the theatre. Even during the sermon some go out, some sleep, and women chatter among themselves about their children. At the least distraction, everybody's attention flies away. There, he says, you are all looking now at the man who lights the lamps!

In the midst of this plain, homely, faithful preaching came the crash of a great tragedy. Theodosius had now been for ten years on the throne of the empire, and he proposed to celebrate the anniversary.

It was the custom on such an imperial occasion to give a donation to the army; every soldier had an addition to his pay. To meet this expense, the emperor announced that a tax would be levied on the larger cities. Of these cities Antioch was one, being the third in the empire for size and wealth. But the Antiochians hated to be taxed. When the proclamation was publicly and officially read it was received for the moment in ominous silence, and then the reading was followed by a riot. The public buildings were attacked by a mad mob. They sacked the splendid Baths of Caligula, cutting the ropes which held the brazen lamps and letting them crash upon the stone floor, even trying to hack down the shade trees in the garden. They invaded the governor's house, and forced their way into his hall of judgment. There stood the statues of the emperor, of the empress lately dead, of the two princes, Honorius and Arcadius, his sons, and of his father. In the clamoring crowd was a boy with a stone; he threw it and hit the image of the emperor. At once, as if some spring of evil magic had been touched, and some devilish incantation had thereby been wrought, the mad mob went wild. They fell upon the imperial statues, broke them into pieces, and proceeded to drag the dismembered stumps through the mud of the streets. In this manner they conducted themselves for three hours. Then they began to consider what they were doing. They began to ask, What will the emperor do?

The offence both of those who had broken and insulted the statues and of those who had not prevented them was enormous. The men would be held guilty of transgression not against the government only, but against heaven. There were many who would remember how in times not long past the emperor of Rome had been regarded not only as a ruler, but as a god. This belief, indeed, had not outlived the change of imperial religion from pagan to Christian, but it still imparted a peculiar quality to the sacred person of the emperor. The governor of Antioch brought his soldiers, and returned to his house from which he had prudently fled. Such of the ringleaders as could be identified were put to death. Men of wealth and position in the city were summoned, examined by torture, deprived of their property by a confiscation which turned their wives and children into the street, and were thrust into the prisons which Libanius had been urging them to reform. Messengers were sent to inform Theodosius at Constantinople, and to ask his will. And following the messengers went Flavian the bishop, a man of eighty years, undertaking in the snows of winter a journey of eight hundred miles to intercede with the Christian emperor for the Christian city. Weeks of suspense followed. Lent came on. The great church where Chrysostom was preaching every day was filled with penitents. All the places of amusement were shut up. The city waited for the decision of the emperor as if it stood before the judgment seat of God.

Under these conditions, Chrysostom preached the Sermons of the Statues.

At first, in the tumult of the calamity, he refrained from preaching. "We have been silent seven days," he says, "even as the friends of Job were." Now he begins to speak: "I mourn now and lament." Lately, he says, we had an earthquake and the walls of our houses were shaken, now our very souls are shaken. "Wherever any one looks abroad, whether upon the columns of the city or upon his neighbors, he seems to see night and deep gloom, so full is all with melancholy. There is a silence big with horror, and loneliness everywhere." "So great a city, the head of those which lie under the eastern sky, now in peril of destruction!" We have indeed insulted a monarch, the summit and head of all the earth. Let us take refuge in the King that is above. Let us call Him to our aid.

Then he exhorts them to put away their sins. He had preached already on the vice of blasphemy, and during these Lenten sermons he refers to it frequently. You were insulting God, he tells them, and thinking that He did not hear or care. Now He has permitted you to insult the emperor, and to come in peril of his anger, that you may understand what your oaths mean. Come, now, put an end to profane language. Let no one go out of this church as he came in, but better! They applauded there, and the preacher cried, "What need have I of these cheers and tumultuous signs of approval? The praise I seek is that ye show forth all I have said in your works." See, he says, how all your wealth is unavailing. Your houses which you have built and adorned at such expense, they cannot deliver you. Build yourselves houses in the heavens.

The bishop sets out on his journey of intercession, and Chrysostom preaches, pointing to his empty seat. He remarks upon his old age, and how he has left his sister at the point of death for their sake. "I know," he says, "that when he has barely seen our pious emperor, and been seen by him, he will be able by his very countenance to allay his wrath. He will take his text from this holy season. He will remind the emperor of that sacred day when Christ remitted the sins of the whole world. He will add that prayer which the emperor was taught when he was admitted to the Holy Communion, 'Forgive us our trespasses, as we forgive those who trespass against us.' He will bring to his memory that in this city the faithful were first called Christians. And the emperor will listen to him. Let us assist him with our prayers; let us supplicate; let us go on embassy to the King that is above with many tears. And remember how it is written of repentant Nineveh, 'God saw their works,'—not their fasting, not their sackcloth; nothing of the sort. 'They turned every one from their evil ways, and the Lord repented of the evil that he had said he would do unto them.' "

Rumors drift to Antioch from Constantinople, now good, now bad: the emperor will do this, the emperor will do that. One time the governor must speak in the church, to reassure the congregation, and dissuade them from fleeing from the city. The monks come down from the surrounding hills to join their prayers and lamentations with the citizens. The messengers return, who had set out before the bishop, and are now back again before he has had an audience with Theodosius. The worst has not befallen the offending city, but it is bad enough. "We expected," says Chrysostom, "innumerable horrors, that the property of all was to be plundered, the houses destroyed together with their inhabitants, the city snatched away from the midst of the world, and all its relics obliterated, and its soil ploughed up." But the emperor was content to degrade Antioch from its metropolitan position, and to close all its places of amusement. I thank God, cries Chrysostom, may they never be reopened!

At last the bishop returned, just before Easter. He had had a conference with the emperor. He had confessed, indeed, the transgression of his people. But he had cited the precedent of Constantine who, when a statue of himself had been pelted with stones, and his whole face, as they said, battered and broken, stroked his face with his hand, and replied smiling, "I do not find the mark of any wound." He had declared that the emperor had it now in his power to set up in his honor the most splendid statue in the world. "For," he said, "if you remit the offences of those who have done you injury, and take no revenge upon them, they will erect a statue to you, not of brass, nor of gold, nor inlaid with gems, but one arrayed in that robe which is more precious than the costliest material, the robe of humanity and tender mercy. Every man will thus set you up in his own soul." To these petitions Theodosius graciously responded. He forgave the city. Go now, says the preacher, at the close of the sermon in which he described the interview, go, light the lamps, and decorate the shops with green, and keep high festival, remembering always to give thanks to God who loveth man.

III

At Constantinople

Ten years of this plain, faithful, and eloquent preaching followed. Then suddenly the scene was changed. The ministry of Chrysostom as presbyter and reformer of the people of Antioch was followed by his ministry as bishop and his vain endeavors to reform the clergy and the court of Constantinople.

The see of Constantinople was vacant. The episcopal chair which Gregory had so suddenly and cheerfully left empty had been filled by the appointment of Nectarius, a rich, courteous, hospitable, and contented person. During the years of his episcopate he had never brought anybody into trouble. He had never seriously interfered in the affairs of the pleasant society in which he lived. Now he was dead. Theodosius was dead also; Arcadius was emperor in the East,—a dull, incapable young man, under the influence of his minister of state, Eutropius the Eunuch.

Eutropius had had an extraordinary history. Born a slave in the valley of the Euphrates, he had grown to manhood in that servile condition, cutting wood, drawing water, and performing the most menial offices. One of his masters had given him as a part of her dowry to his daughter. His business was to comb her hair and fan her with a fan of peacock's feathers. Growing now old and wrinkled, and his mistress becoming weary of the sight of him, she tried to sell him.

Being unable to find a purchaser at any price she turned him into the street. After a time of the direst poverty, living on the scraps which he got by begging at back doors, he found a job in the emperor's kitchen. Here he was so fortunate as to attract the attention of Theodosius. Thus he crept from one step to another till he became chamberlain of the palace. In this position he advanced his own interests and enfeebled the young Arcadius by surrounding him with debasing pleasures. At last came the day when Arcadius was to marry the daughter of his prime minister, Rufinus. The procession set out in splendor from the palace to the house of the bride. But it passed the house without stopping; it proceeded to the residence of Bauto the Frank, and there Arcadius was married to his daughter, Eudoxia! This was the work of Eutropius, who thereupon succeeded Rufinus, having first assisted in his murder, and became minister of state.

It is one of the most singular careers in history. The palace gates would open and out would ride a resplendent procession of foot-soldiers in white uniforms, of cavalry in cloth of gold, with gilded lances and golden shields, and then, drawn by white mules, the imperial carriage, with gilded sides shining like the sun, and in the carriage by the side of the emperor, the old ex-slave Eutropius.

Now the archbishopric of Constantinople was vacant, the most important see in Christendom, next to Rome, and, in the mind of the East, exceeding Rome. There was a long array of candidates. In the midst of the discussion Eutropius remembered Chrysostom, whom he had heard preach. He sent secretly to Antioch. By falsehood his messengers got Chrysostom into a carriage, swift horses were ready, and against his will, not even asking what his will was, under guard like a criminal condemned to execution, the preacher was carried to Constantinople. Theophilus, the Pope of Alexandria, was commanded to consecrate him.

But Theophilus was reluctant, having a candidate of his own, who, he hoped, would assist him in asserting the superiority of the see of Alexandria over the see of Constantinople. This reluctance Eutropius was able to overcome. For in the late war between Theodosius and Maximin, when the issue of the combat was uncertain, and nobody could tell which of the two would win the imperial throne, Theophilus had sent two letters to the field of battle, one congratulating Theodosius, the other congratulating Maximin, upon his victory. One was to be delivered to the conqueror, the other was to be destroyed. But the other letter had not been destroyed; it was in the possession of Eutropius. So persuasive was the argument which Eutropius based upon this unfortunate epistle, that Theophilus agreed to consecrate Chrysostom. And this he did, but with a hatred in his heart which entered tragically into the years which followed.

Thus Chrysostom became the bishop of Constantinople,—the archbishop, the patriarch, the pope, of the imperial capital of the East. The whole occupation of his life was changed. He still preached, but not, as in Antioch, day after day; sometimes as rarely as only once in a month. He was mainly engaged in the unaccustomed duties of administration. And his preaching, which in Antioch had been addressed to people who had known him from his youth, and which had been reinforced by the common knowledge of his holy life, was now the voice not only of a stranger but of a suspected stranger, thrust violently into his position by old Eutropius whom everybody feared and hated. He was Eutropius's bishop.

The first thing which Chrysostom did was to take all the fine furniture which Nectarius, his elegant predecessor, had gathered in the episcopal palace, and have it sold at auction, giving the money to a hospital. He dismissed the retinue of servants. The pleasant hospitality of the bishop's residence he discontinued; he stopped the dinner parties which had made Nectarius so popular. He lived alone and dined alone, in the dismantled rooms. One bishop who visited him was made a formidable enemy by the hard bed and the homely breakfast, which he regarded as a personal insult.

This ideal of monastic simplicity, Chrysostom demanded of his clergy. He interfered with their domestic arrangements, which were in some instances a cause of scandal. He tried to dissuade rich parishioners from giving presents to the rich clergy, urging them to remember the poor. Some priests he suspended, some he thrust out of their positions; almost all of them he reprimanded for their comfortable habits and their neglect of duty. Thus they were set against him. At the same time he offended the bishops. In the course of a single visitation he deposed thirteen of them. He found Constantinople infested with idle monks, living on the charity of industrious citizens; he sent them back to their cells. Thus he daily increased the number of his enemies.

Wherever Chrysostom went, he measured the church by the standard of his own consecrated life, and punished declension from that high ideal. The church was secularized: anybody could see that. The conversion of Constantine had given the Christian religion a most unfortunate popularity, and many were they who had entered the church because it was in favor with the court; and being in the church, even in the holy offices of presbyter and bishop, they were behaving more like courtiers than like Christians. It was a lax, indifferent, pleasure-loving church, in which conscience afforded only a weak defence against temptation. And over the church, ruling it in the name of Christ, and holding himself responsible for it, was a man who had spent half of his mature life as a monk, and the other half as a preacher of austere morals.

To the clerical enmity which such a situation made inevitable, he had the misfortune to add the hostility of the ladies of Constantinople. The preacher is safe who denounces in large, general terms the sins of avarice and luxury, but he comes into immediate peril when he proceeds to particulars. Chrysostom proceeded to particulars. With the unwisdom of one who lives apart from common life, he confused small things with great. He prejudiced his cause, and needlessly made personal enemies in his congregation, by criticising in his sermons the fashions of their dress. He objected to the ladies' earrings, and to their white veils with black filets. He disliked their shoes of velvet laced with silk, which he said they might better wear upon their heads. He pointed at them with his finger: "You women there in the silk dresses are laughing." He said plainly that there were old women in the congregation who were dressing like young girls. He declared that he would repel from the Holy Communion any woman who came with painted cheeks.

The familiar prayer of St. Chrysostom is so named because it was taken over into the English service out of the Greek Liturgy of St. Chrysostom. This Liturgy, according to which the Holy Communion is administered to this day in the Orthodox Eastern Church, is a revision of an earlier form called the Liturgy of St. Basil, as that in turn was recast from the traditional Liturgy of St. James. Whether Chrysostom contributed to this revision, or whether the name was given to it by reason of his fame, has not been determined.

The only record of a connection of Chrysostom with the worship of the church is made by the ecclesiastical historian Socrates (book vi, chap. 8). He says that the Arians began to reassert themselves in Constantinople during the episcopate of Chrysostom, and that being forbidden to have churches within the city walls they had them just outside, and attracted congregations to them by processional singing. They met in the public squares and sang hymns which Socrates calls "responsive compositions," perhaps with a chorus after each verse, and thus gathering a crowd, they proceeded to their churches. In opposition to these heretical meetings Chrysostom organized the orthodox choirs, which, by the generosity of Eudoxia, he provided with silver crosses on which they bore wax candles. This competition proved so effective that one evening the singing heretics fell upon the singing orthodox, and there was a fight in the street, with silver crosses converted into clubs, and much injurious throwing of stones. This occasioned the stopping of all the processional invitations to the services.

The dramatic interest of the sermons which Chrysostom preached in Antioch on the statues was equaled in Constantinople by his sermons on Eutropius.

Eutropius was now the acting emperor, controlling the weak Arcadius, and doing as he pleased. He had cast down, and exiled or put to death great generals and officers of state. Out of the imperial kitchen he had taken a servant, a friend of his in the days of his poverty, and had made him a person of exalted station. Statues were erected to Eutropius in all the greater cities, while men were still living who had bought and sold and beaten him. Naturally, he was hated. He had many enemies among the nobility into whose aristocratic ranks he had been so singularly thrust, and toward whom he behaved with unfailing arrogance. He had incurred the displeasure of the people by his failure to keep peace with the Goths, and by the open avarice of his appointments. They said that he had a price-list of governorships: so much to be made governor of Pontus, so much to be made governor of Galatia. His one friend was the queen, whose marriage he had so dramatically managed.

But Eutropius quarrelled with the queen. One day when she declined some demand of his, "Remember," he said, "that he who placed you where you are is able to remove you." The young queen took her little children, one of them two years old and the other a baby, and ran crying to her husband. And Arcadius, by a rare exercise of his will, asserted himself. He discharged Eutropius. In one moment, in the speaking of a single sentence, he toppled over his whole pile of power, and turned him out of the palace. Out he went, poor as when he came in, and without a friend. He fled to the cathedral, pursued by a mob of soldiers and citizens. He took refuge under the altar. Chrysostom stood at the entrance to the sanctuary and refused them entrance.

The next day was Sunday, and when the time came for Chrysostom's sermon, and he gave out his text, "Vanity of vanities, all is vanity!" he had the curtain drawn aside which hid the altar from the people, and there clinging to the sacred table was the old, wrinkled, gray-haired Eutropius. "Where now," cried the preacher, "are the brilliant surroundings of thy consulship? Where are the gleaming torches? Where is the applause which greeted thee in the city, where the acclamation in the hippodrome? They are gone—all gone. A wind has blown upon the tree, shattering down all its leaves. Where now are your feigned friends? Where are your drinking parties and your suppers? Where is the wine that used to be poured forth all day long, and the manifold dainties invented by your cooks? They were a smoke which has dispersed, bubbles which have burst, cobwebs which have been rent in pieces. 'Vanity of vanities, all is vanity.' " "Brethren," added the preacher, "I have told you that, a thousand times: I have declared to you that wealth and the pleasures of this life are fleeting things. Look now, and see with your own eyes, how what I said is true."

The life of Eutropius was saved for the moment by the intercession of Chrysostom, but he was finally beheaded.

The sermons on Eutropius mark the culmination of the power of Chrysostom in Constantinople. After these discourses, in which he twice "improved the occasion" of the downfall of the favorite, little remains but disappointment, and hostility, and final failure. His clerical enemies found a leader in Theophilus of Alexandria; his social enemies were encouraged by the empress Eudoxia.

Theophilus took as a pretext for an attack upon Chrysostom the case of the Four Tall Brothers. These were monks of Egypt who had come into collision with Theophilus over the orthodoxy of Origen. Theophilus held Origen to be a heretic, and forbade the reading of his writings. This edict was disobeyed by independent persons whose liking for Origen was emphasized by the bishop's peremptory displeasure. Among these disobedient persons were the Four Tall Brothers, who finding themselves in peril fled to Constantinople to plead for the protection of the court.

Their hospitable reception by Chrysostom gave Theophilus his opportunity. He appeared in Constantinople with a stout-armed retinue of Egyptian clergy, allied himself with the multitude of clerical malcontents in the city, and at a country place belonging to the emperor, and called The Oak, situated near by in Chalcedon, he proceeded to summon a synod. This Synod of the Oak, under the presidency of Theophilus, called Chrysostom to present himself for trial, and, when he denied the jurisdiction of the assembly and refused to plead, deposed him.

It was a situation which a man of the world would have met by beating the intruders over the head with their own weapons. Cyprian, for example, or Ambrose, or any other strong bishop who had prepared himself for the ministry by serving an apprenticeship as a lawyer or a statesman, would have confronted Theophilus and his clerical ruffians at the docks when they landed, and would have driven them back into their boats. And if the emperor or the empress, with the whole court in agreement, had interposed in their behalf, he would have brought to his defence and reinforcement an excommunication which they would have dreaded like the onslaught of a legion of angels.

But Chrysostom was a gentle spirit, bold in the pulpit, but unfitted by his monastic training to deal with the rough world. He knew how to speak, but his experience had never taught him how to act. The situation was complicated by the fact that Theophilus had got permission from the emperor to summon the assembly. Disobedience to its decision—so they told Chrysostom—was nothing less than treason. He bowed, therefore, to what seemed inevitable and submitted to an imperial decree of banishment. Theophilus "ejected me," says Chrysostom, "from the city and the church, when the evening was far advanced. Being drawn by the public informer through the midst of the city, and dragged along by force, I was taken down to the sea, and thrust on board a ship."

The city was profoundly stirred. Chrysostom had been the friend of the poor; he had built hospitals; he had himself lived in poverty that he might thereby be more helpful to his people; he had maintained the cause of Christian righteousness. Everybody, whether friend or enemy, knew the self-sacrificing, devoted, humble-minded goodness of the bishop. Everybody knew also that out of envy, and for purposes of personal ambition, without a shadow of justice and in defiance of religion, Theophilus had come from Alexandria to ruin him. The amazement of the people deepened into indignation. It was unsafe for any Egyptian to be seen in the streets. A mob besieged the palace of the emperor. The next night there was an earthquake. Especially in the palace the walls swayed, and the roof seemed about to fall. Eudoxia was thoroughly frightened. She sent for Chrysostom with tears and apologies. The people met him as if he had been a commander returning from the conquest of a nation; a triumphal procession bore him to the cathedral and seated him upon his throne. At midnight Theophilus, fearing for his life, took his company with him and got on board a boat, and so escaped.

Then two months passed. The earth resumed its accustomed steadiness, the panic of fright was forgotten in the palace and the old hostility returned. The ambition of Theophilus was succeeded by the opposition of Eudoxia.

As the natural leader of the society against which Chrysostom had preached, the empress had felt herself personally aggrieved. She wore the fine clothes to which the bishop had objected, and lived the life of luxury which he had declared to be contrary to right religion. One day, she had a silver statue of herself set on a pillar of porphyry in the midst of the square beside which stood the Church of Santa Sophia. The event was celebrated on a Sunday, and at a time when there was service in the church. The din of the affair was deafening. Against the noise of the shouting and the blare of the trumpets the choir found it impossible to sing. Chrysostom found it impossible to preach. Indeed, there was little occasion for a sermon, most of the congregation being outside in the crowd.

Chrysostom discussed the matter with his usual plainness of speech. And this plainness was by no means modified in the reports which were carried to the empress. They told her that he compared her not only with Jezebel, but with Herodias. They said that he began a sermon with the words, "Again is Herodias furious; again Herodias dances; again does she demand the head of John." Chrysostom declared that he never said it; it is plain that no attentive reader of the Bible would speak of the dancing of Herodias. But any pretext was enough.

Another council was assembled, ready to do the will of Theophilus, and protected by a force of barbarians imported for the purpose. This council confirmed the previous sentence, and declared Chrysostom deposed because after that condemnation he had resumed his duties without permission. On Easter

Even, soldiers broke into the churches, and drove out the clergy and the congregation, and dispersed those who had come in white robes to be baptized. The baptismal pools were made red with blood. On the day of the great festival the churches of Constantinople stood empty, the faithful having fled to the fields. "There were shrieks and lamentations," says Chrysostom, "and torrents of tears were shed everywhere in the marketplaces, in the houses, in the deserts; all places were in a state of tumult and confusion as if the city had been taken by an enemy." Hostile bishops led the attack, preceded by drill-sergeants, says Chrysostom, instead of deacons.

IV

In Exile

The decree of banishment was now executed without repentance. Chrysostom was hurried into a boat on the Bosphorus and carried into exile. As they set sail, and the bishop looked back upon the city to which he had been brought so dramatically and from which he was being thrust so violently, behold, smoke and flame began to rise from the roof of the cathedral. Santa Sophia, even as they watched, fell into a heap of blazing ruins. The wreck of the fallen walls was piled high over the silver statue of Eudoxia.

In the parallelogram of Asia Minor, between the Black Sea and the Mediterranean, Constantinople is just outside the northwest corner. Chrysostom was banished to Cucusus in the southeast corner. The long journey involved not only the ordinary difficulties of travel in a mountainous country, but also the peril of Isaurian brigands who were then infesting the roads. To the distress of mind caused by daily reports of the persecution of the faithful in Constantinople was added pain of body; and the common dangers of the journey were accompanied and embittered by the hatred of ecclesiastical enemies. Chrysostom wrote to Olympias, a deaconess, describing his experiences at Cæsarea. He says that he arrived there late one evening, in an exhausted condition, in the height of a burning fever, more dead than alive. The next day the Isaurians besieged the city. At the same time a great rabble of monks, perhaps driven from their cells by the marauders, attacked the house in which Chrysostom was lodged, and tried to set fire to it. They said openly that they had the approval of the bishop of Cæsarea. At midnight, in the blackness of darkness, for there was no moon, a cry was made that the Isaurians were coming. Chrysostom was forced from his sick-bed. It was unsafe to light a torch for fear of the barbarians. The mule on which he rode stumbled and threw him. "Imagine my sufferings," he writes, "encompassed as I was by such calamities, oppressed by the fever, ignorant of the plans which had been made, in terror of the barbarians, and trembling with the expectation of falling into their hands." Nevertheless, he went forward, and after a month reached Cucusus.

There he spent three years. He wrote letters to influential bishops,—at Aquileia, at Milan, at Rome, —

calling their attention to the injustice with which he had been treated. "Not even in heathen courts," he wrote, "would such audacious deeds have been committed, or rather not even in a barbarian court: neither Scythian nor Sarmatians would ever have judged a cause in this fashion, deciding it after hearing one side only, in the absence of the accused, who only deprecated enmity, not a trial of his case, who was ready to call any number of witnesses, asserting himself to be innocent and able to clear himself of the charges in the face of the world."

But neither Pope Innocent nor anybody else could help him. He was under condemnation for the offence of attacking the corruption of the church and of society. His plain preaching had got him the hatred of the imperial court. And these combined forces were too strong for him. When friends began to gather about him from Antioch, so that it was said, "All Antioch is at Cucusus," the authorities at Constantinople determined to send him to a remoter exile. He was to be hurried north to Pityus on the Black Sea.

But in Pontus, near Comana, he became so ill that further progress was impossible. He was taken to the wayside shrine of Basilicus, a bishop who had suffered martyrdom. There he died, being in his sixtieth year. It was said that his last words were, "Glory be to God for all things!"

Thus he died, and the glory of the Eastern Church died with him. Athanasius, Basil, Gregory, Chrysostom had no successors. Not another name of eminence appears in the ecclesiastical annals of the

Eastern Empire. In the contest for the mastery of human life, the court had conquered; the church was brought into subjection.

CHAPTER IX

MONASTICISM IN THE WEST: MARTIN, CASSIAN AND JEROME

I

East and West

The statement that "East is East and West is West, and never the twain shall meet," is based on racial differences. Some of these are superficial, and find expression in the extraordinary contrasts between the Oriental and the Occidental ways of doing things. But others are temperamental. The East is the land of meditation, where men think for the joy of thinking, and do not require that their thoughts shall tend toward any concrete conclusion. The West is the land of action.

The meditative man desires to withdraw from the world. He seeks a place of quiet where he may escape the manifold distractions of common life; he subordinates the body to the spirit; he dreams of an ideal state for which this present life is a preparation or probation. He believes in a "world-renouncing ethic," whose formula is "We live to die."

The active man desires to use and control the world. His happiness is to immerse himself in affairs. He is forever busy with investigation, and with the problem of applying the results of investigation to the conditions of life. He takes the planet as it stands, and is glad that he is a citizen of it; he would make the most of all his opportunities. He believes in a "world-affirming ethic," whose formula is "We live to live."

It is easy to exaggerate the contrast between the mind of the East and the mind of the West. Human nature laughs at generalizations. Two great religions of the East have contradicted the doctrine that we live to die. Confucius said nothing about the gods, Moses said nothing about the life to come. These religions, in the heart of the East, concerned themselves with the present life. The teachings of Confucius were as practical as the teachings of Franklin. The historians, the poets and the prophets of Judaism agreed that the rewards and punishments of God are to be looked for in this world, and appear in health and in sickness, in prosperity and in adversity.

Indeed, the East and the West have twice met already. They met in Greek philosophy, where the Stoics regarded the world from the point of view which we consider characteristically Eastern, and their neighbors the Epicureans regarded life from the point of view which seems to us distinctively Western. They met also in the Christian religion, whose essential adjectives are the words "spiritual" and "social." Jesus taught a love of God which includes all that is Oriental in its renunciation of the world, and a love of man which in its affirmation of the world includes all that is Occidental.

The contrast, however, between the East and the West is real and abiding. It is true that the difference between the monastic ideal of Basil and the monastic ideal of Benedict is surprisingly slight. Basil is as practical as Benedict, and makes quite as much of the life of action: he sets his monks to till the ground and to apply themselves to reading and writing. The fact remains, however, that Eastern monasticism and Western monasticism took different roads, and have had a very different history: largely because the Eastern monks were Orientals and the Western monks were Occidentals. The racial differences appeared.

Eastern monasticism renounced the world: at first by way of protest, then by way of frank despair. At first the Eastern monks came back occasionally to express their opinion of the world. They swarmed out of the deserts into the streets of the cities in which the bishops were sitting in council, and denounced heretics and sinners. Sometimes they were in the right; more often, in the wrong. Their monastic seclusion had made them ignorant fanatics. But gradually they ceased to take even an occasional part in the affairs of the world. They turned their backs upon it in despair. They shut themselves up behind their high stone walls and let the world go by. In the monotony of their regulated life there was no place for individual expression. Their annals no longer showed great names. They were connected with the church only by the fact that the bishops were selected from their brotherhood. But the bishops came from the monasteries unacquainted with the life of the lay world, and unfitted to take any influential part in it. Far from continuing the original protest, they were submissive servants of the state.

In Western monasticism, on the other hand, the monks developed the institution by the continual assertion of individuality. Their history is filled with the names of those who were leaders of their generation. And these leaders, for the most part, showed their leadership by their defiance of uniformity. The monks contended with the bishops, perpetuating the initial protest against the conventionality and secularity of the church. They contended among themselves, and thereby made their history a series of notable reforms, each of which made the monastic ideal higher and wider than before. And they controlled the world. They had such part in it that no history of Europe can be adequately written without including them.

The three outstanding names of the monastic movement in the West are St. Martin, St. John Cassian, and St. Jerome. Each promoted the new life in his own way: Martin by his example, Cassian by teaching the West the methods of the East, Jerome by a propaganda which amazed and startled the society of Rome.

II

Martin

The disciple and biographer of St. Martin, Sulpicius Severus, begins his book with a preface addressed to his friend Desiderius to whom he entrusts it. I had determined, he says, to keep this little treatise private. I am sending it to you because you have asked me for it so many times, but on the understanding that you will not show it to anybody else: remember, you promised me that. At the same time, I have my fears that in spite of my entreaty and your promise you will nevertheless publish it. If you do, please ask the readers to pay more attention to the facts which are here related than to the imperfect language in which they are set forth; remind them that the kingdom of God consists not of eloquence, but of faith, and that the gospel was preached not by orators, but by fishermen. Or, better still, when you publish the book, erase my name from the title-page, that the book may proclaim its subject-matter, while it tells nothing of the author.

Thus we are made acquainted with the pleasant and modest person whose account of St. Martin is the only considerable source of information concerning him.

Martin was the son of pagan parents, in Pannonia, where his father was a military tribune. In his early childhood he was attracted toward the Christian Church,—so much so that when he was but twelve years of age, he made up his mind to be a hermit. This intention his father hindered, and three years later, upon the occasion of an edict which required that the sons of veterans should be enrolled for military service, he sent him, much against young Martin's will, into the army. There Martin tried to follow his vocation by changing places with his servant, whose boots he insisted upon cleaning. It was evident to all his associates that the warfare in which this soldier was concerned was directed not against the Goths, but against the devil. To this statement Sulpicius adds that all his companions marvellously loved him.

Then one day in the midst of a fierce winter, when there was much suffering among the poor, Martin met at the gate of Amiens a shivering beggar. Thereupon he took off his military cloak, cut it into two pieces with his sword, and put one half upon the beggar's back. That night in a dream Christ appeared to Martin wearing the half of the severed cloak and saying to a multitude of angels, "Martin, who is still but a catechumen, clothed me with this robe." In consequence of this dream Martin was baptized, being then about twenty years of age.

Presently, when the commander of the army reviewed the troops on the eve of a battle with the barbarians, Martin took the opportunity to ask that he might be relieved of his military duties in order to devote himself to the religious life. "I am the soldier of Christ," he said, "it is not lawful for me to fight." When the commander, naturally enough, accused him of cowardice, he offered to go into the battle on the morrow, wholly unarmed and without the protection of shield or helmet, at the head of the army, if after that he might be dismissed. That night the barbarians

decided that the odds were too much against them, and the next day they surrendered. And Martin was set free.

Entering thus upon a life devoted to religion, Martin found that his new career offered him quite as many opportunities for adventure as the old. Once, in the Alps, he was attacked by robbers, and was in peril of his life. One of the robbers had his axe uplifted to strike Martin, when another stopped him. This kindly brigand Martin converted. "Who are you?" said the brigand. "I am a Christian," said Martin.—"Are you not afraid?"—"I have never been more sure of my safety in my life. But I am afraid for you: you are in danger of everlasting damnation." Sulpicius had the story from a hermit, whom he found to be the converted robber himself.

Once as he prayed, the place where Martin was kneeling was filled with a glory of purple light, and there appeared one crowned with gold and clad in a royal robe. And the vision said, "Martin, I am the Lord Christ, at last descended out of heaven to earth, and manifested first of all to you." And Martin, instructed by long experience, at first kept silence, till the vision said again, "Martin, do you not believe?" To which the saint replied, "The Lord Jesus never promised to return in purple, with a crown upon his head. Where are the prints of the nails?" At the sound of these words the defeated devil vanished.

Martin suffered much from many enemies, natural and supernatural.

He was reviled by those who felt that his holy life was a criticism upon themselves. Sulpicius says, "Some of his calumniators, although very few, some of his maligners, I say, were reported to be bishops!" The biographer is reluctant to recall the names of any of these injurious ecclesiastics.

"I shall deem it sufficient," he says, "that, if any of them reads this account and perceives that he is himself pointed at, he may have the grace to blush. But if, on the other hand, he shows anger, he will, by that very fact, own that he is among those spoken of, though all the time perhaps I may have been thinking of some other person."

This enmity of officials was the natural result of Martin's increasing influence. He was beginning to disturb the conscience of the contented church. He was exhibiting in his life of renunciation an ideal which contrasted sharply with the lax and secular religion of the time. It was an ideal which devout souls recognized and which they desired to follow. Sulpicius says that when he visited Martin, the saint continually insisted that the allurements of the world and all secular burdens are to be abandoned that one may be free and unencumbered in serving the Lord Jesus. Sulpicius abandoned them. Paulinus of Nola, a great nobleman, forsook his splendid house and his fair estate on the Garonne, and the pleasant society in which he lived, to follow Martin into the solitude of the woods. It made a profound sensation in the Roman world. Many others undertook the ascetic life.

Martin was thus the Antony of the West, the pioneer of an unorganized monasticism, attracting men by the fascination of his holy life, but leaving them for the most part to use such spiritual methods as they pleased. His settlement near Poictiers, in 360, almost coincident with the monastic life of Basil and Gregory, was probably the first monastery in Europe. The Life of Martin which Sulpicius wrote became a kind of monastic gospel, like the Life of Antony written by Athanasius. It was read everywhere. It was the most popular book of the fourth century.

Martin was like Antony in his belief that he was visited by devils; whom, however, he encountered without fear. He had even a kindly feeling for the chief of the devils, to whom he once ventured to promise salvation, if he would but repent him of his sins.

The people of Tours called Martin from his prayers and meditations to be their bishop. They had to deceive him to get him from his monastery. One of them pretended that his wife was desperately ill, and begged him to come and visit her. Then they all crowded about him, and he was made bishop in spite of himself. He went on foot about his vast diocese, preaching from town to town, contending with paganism, destroying idols, converting the heathen, and everywhere winning the love and reverence of men. He was the evangelist of France; the apostle to the Gauls.

He never ceased to be a monk. Two miles out of Tours, beside the river Loire, he found a retreat so secret and retired that he was able to hide himself in it. It was like the glen of Annesi as described by Basil. "On one side it was surrounded by a precipitous rock of a lofty mountain, while the Loire had shut in the rest of the plain by a bay extending back for a little distance; and the place could be approached only by a single passage, and that a very narrow one." But even in this concealment he was discovered. Young men, like-minded with him, found him out, and settled near him in caves of the overhanging mountain, till there were eighty of them, meeting daily for prayer and having their meals in common, clothed in garments of camel's hair.

Once Martin appeared at the court of the emperor Maximus, to intercede for the Priscillianists. These were gentle, enthusiastic and mistaken persons who had fallen into a heresy concerning which we are informed only by references in the writings of their enemies. The descriptions sound like a sort of gnosticism. The Priscillianists were educated and even literary persons, and some of them were rich. They were attacked by two neighboring bishops, regarding whose bad character even the orthodox accounts agree. These bishops gathered a council of their brethren and condemned the heretics. They appealed to the emperor, and the emperor was about to confirm the condemnation when Martin appeared. He had no inclination toward the errors of the Priscillianists, but he knew that their lives were innocent and holy. In response to his intercession the emperor promised to set them free. Hardly was the saint's back turned, however, when the angry bishops persuaded the emperor and he had Priscillian beheaded, with six of his companions. The event is memorable as the first formal handing over of a condemned heretic to a secular court for punishment. It was the beginning of a long series of shameful tragedies.

Martin indignantly protested, and at first refused to hold communion with the offending bishops. In order, however, to save the lives of some of the lesser members of the sect, he felt it necessary to yield. He attended a synod of bishops, and he dined at the table of the emperor. It is said that when the wine was passed to him, and he was expected to pass it to the emperor, he gave it to his chaplain, thus declaring that the humblest priest is above the proudest prince. So, at least, the incident was interpreted in a day when the church was contending with the state for the mastery of the world. As for the bishops, St. Martin declared that if God would forgive him for sitting with them in that synod, he would never attend another. He was of the mind of St. Gregory of Nazianzus regarding ecclesiastical conventions.

"No one ever saw him enraged or excited," says Sulpicius, "or lamenting or laughing; he was always one and the same, displaying a kind of heavenly happiness in his countenance. Never was there a feeling in his heart except piety, peace and tender mercy." The cape which he wore—*capella*—became one of the most precious possessions of the kings of France, and the sanctuary which was built to contain it was called Capella, hence our word chapel. The position of his memorial day in the church calendar gives to the most beautiful weeks of autumn the name of St. Martin's Summer.

III

Cassian

When Martin died, in the year 400, John Cassian was completing the second of two long visits to the monasteries of Egypt. Cassian was a man of the West, probably of Gaul. His well-to-do parents had given him an excellent education, which had so filled his memory with the words of the classic authors that they frequently came in between him and the sacred page. He could not read the accounts of the battles and heroes of the books of Kings and Chronicles without remembering Homer, and with the verses of the Psalms he heard the choruses of Æschylus.

He was still young, however, when the passion for the ascetic life possessed him. There being then no monasteries in his native land, he made his way to the East, a pioneer of those who, long after, out of the same country, journeyed as pilgrims or crusaders to the Christian shrines of Palestine. He settled among monks in Bethlehem. But Cassian had a hungry mind. He was not content to say his prayers and save his soul. He would be not a monk only, but a student of monasticism. He made himself familiar, accordingly, with the monastic methods first of Bethlehem, and then of Syria, and asked permission to visit the famous communities of Egypt. Leave for such a journey was given on the condition of a speedy return, and Cassian and his friend Germanus started on their voyage of discovery.

They landed on the Delta of the Nile, and proceeded immediately to visit the holy hermits who had their dwelling in the salt marshes. They interviewed old Chæremon, now past his hundredth year, who had prayed so continuously that he could no longer stand up straight, but went upon his hands and knees. He preached to the young visitors on Perfection and on the Protection of God; and on these sermons, as on all the other discourses which they heard, they took notes. The Abbot Pinufius preached on the Marks of Satisfaction. The Abbot John told them how having been a hermit he had left that solitary life and entered a community in order to practise the virtues of subjection and obedience. The Abbot Abraham instructed them on Mortification. The pilgrims were now so heartily enjoying themselves, and were finding their visit so profitable, that they reflected with much regret upon the pledge which they had given to return to Bethlehem after a few weeks. They consulted the Abbot Joseph, who explained to them the Obligation of Promises. The explanation was so satisfactory that they continued on their travels and did not return to Bethlehem till after seven years.

Even then, they remained but a short time among the brethren, being again permitted by them to go to Egypt, where they continued their monastic explorations. They now visited the Nitrian Valley, in the Libyan desert, northwest of Cairo, a place filled with monasteries. Dr. Butler, who visited the district in 1883, found four of these groups of buildings still standing and inhabited. They were all constructed on the same plan, and the general appearance of them to-day probably differs little from what Cassian found. Each is described as "a veritable fortress, standing about one hundred and fifty yards square, with blind, lofty walls rising sheer out of the sand. Each monastery has also, either detached or not, a large keep, or tower, standing four-square, and approached only by a drawbridge. The tower contains the library, storerooms for the vestments and sacred vessels, cellars for oil and corn, and many strange holes and hiding-places for the monks in the last resort, if their citadel should be taken by the enemy. Within the monastery are enclosed one principal and one or two smaller court-yards, around which stand the cells of the monks, domestic buildings, such as the mill-room, the oven, the refectory, and the like, and the churches."

In such monasteries, and in the retreats of hermits, Cassian and his friend were privileged to listen to the discourses of holy men, which they recorded as they had done among the monks of the Delta. The Abbot Serenus, who spoke of Inconstancy of Mind and of Spiritual Wickedness, taught them that the way to holiness is beset by continual temptation; and the teaching was confirmed by Serapion, who instructed them in the "Eight Principal Faults" of the monastic life: gluttony, fornication, covetousness, anger, dejection, vain-glory and pride,—being in large part the sins to escape which the monks had fled into the desert,—

together with a new sin which they found waiting for them there, the sin called "accidie," meaning literally "without care," "without interest," the sin of religious indifference. It overtook them in the midst of their prayers and fastings, this desperate question as to the value of it all. They wearied of their holy living; for the moment, they hated it. They described this fault, in the phrase of a psalm, as "the sickness that destroyeth in the noonday." The sun of the African desert beat upon their heads, and their hearts failed within them. All their painful life of renunciation and devotion seemed a wicked folly.

After these profitable travels Cassian went to Constantinople, where he found Chrysostom undergoing persecution. He took the side of the saint, by whom he was presently ordained; and it was he who carried to Rome the letter of the faithful, describing the scandalous manner in which Chrysostom had been deposed and exiled. From Rome he went to the neighborhood of Marseilles, and there in the midst of a dense, primeval forest he established two monasteries, one for men and one for women. These he organized according to the patterns which he had studied in the East.

At Marseilles, he wrote the two books which gave him a place in the history of monasticism in the West corresponding to the place of St. Basil in the history of monasticism in the East. He found monastic enthusiasm and a passion for the ascetic life; and he found men, inspired by the examples of Martin, of Hilary of Poictiers and of Paulinus of Nola, living solitary or in communities engaged in prayer. But all this was informal, unconnected and without regulation.

Cassian's "institutes," describing the life which the monks lived in Egypt, brought the experience of the East to the service of the West. He gave a detailed account of the dress of the monks, their sheepskins and goatskins, their hoods and girdles, even their shoes. He explained how they arranged and kept their hours of prayer. He called attention to the reverence and serenity of their devotions. "When the psalm is ended," he said, "they do not hurry at once to kneel down, as some of us do in this country, who, before the psalm is fairly ended, make haste to prostrate themselves for prayer, in their hurry to finish the service as quickly as possible." He glorified the obedience of the Abbot John, who at the command of a superior stuck a dry stick into the ground, and for the space of a whole year watered it twice a day with water which he drew from the river two miles distant; and the obedience of the Abbot Patermucius, who having brought with him into the desert his little boy of eight, carried him in his arms to the river, as Abraham had conducted Isaac to the mountain, and, being so ordered, threw him in; whom the brethren, we are glad to learn, pulled safely out.

These "Institutes" St. Benedict afterwards made the basis of his famous Rule, declaring his purpose not to improve on Cassian, but to adapt his plans to the actual level of ordinary human nature. Thus they underlie to-day the order of the monastic life wherever it is practised in the West. Cassian's "Conferences," also called "Collations," being the notes which he took of the sermons of the holy brethren, Benedict arranged to have read daily in his monasteries, page by page. In the late afternoon, after the day's work was done, Benedict's monks sat in the cloister while one read aloud the discourses which Cassian had collected, and the supper of fruit which followed was called the collation, from the reading.

IV

Jerome

The pilgrimage of Cassian was not a unique experience. Others were taking similar journeys of holy adventure. The biographer of St. Martin gives an account of a French monk, Postumianus, who sailed to Carthage to worship at the tomb of Cyprian, and then, being driven by a contrary wind upon a barren coast of Africa, found a hermit in a desert, who, he says, served him a truly luxurious breakfast, "consisting of the half of a barley cake." Thence he went to Alexandria where he found monks and bishops debating disgracefully over the writings of Origen. No sight, however, interested him more than the spectacle of a monk of Bethlehem, who, says the traveller, "is always occupied in reading, always at his books with his whole heart; he takes no rest day or night: he is perpetually either reading or writing something." This monk was St. Jerome.

Jerome was born in Pannonia, the native land of Martin. The place of his birth was soon after destroyed by the advancing barbarians, and his parents were killed. He was educated in Rome, where his Latin teacher was old Ælius Donatus, whose grammar ("Ars Grammatica") was taught in the schools for a thousand years. This was the schoolmaster whom Dante found conversing with Chrysostom in Paradise. As Cassian remembered his Homer and Æschylus, so Jerome remembered his Cicero and Plautus. One time, long after, he was carried in a dream before the Judgment Seat above. The judge said, "Who are you?" Jerome replied, "I am a Christian." "No," said the judge, "you are a Ciceronian." And the angels were commanded to beat him. He says that when he waked his shoulders were black and blue.

Jerome entered, like Tertullian and Augustine at Carthage, into the immoralities of Rome, and was never free, in all his life, from the temptations of the flesh. But he was converted. He went at once into asceticism. At Aquileia a group of friends gathered about him, and they lived together under discipline, saying their prayers, and discussing religion. The affection which these men had for Jerome ought to be remembered over against his later quarrels and controversies. It was said of him, indeed, that he never hesitated to sacrifice a friend for an opinion; but he had at the same time a genius for friendship. He was mightily attractive to these companions, as afterwards to many good women in Rome. They admired and loved him. Presently the group set out together on a pilgrimage to the East. After wanderings which brought them to Antioch, Jerome fell sick, and so continued for a year. Two of his friends died.

Recovering, and being now alone, he went into a neighboring desert, a refuge of monks and hermits, where he stayed for five years. Here his austerities did but increase the sensual temptations which he was seeking to escape. "I used to sit alone," says Jerome. "I had no companions but scorpions and wild beasts. Sackcloth disfigured my limbs, and my skin from long neglect had grown as black as an Ethiopian's. Tears and groans were every day my portion; and if drowsiness chanced to overcome my struggles against it, my bare bones, which hardly held together, clashed against the ground. Yet how often in that vast solitude, in that savage dwelling-place, parched by a burning sun, how often did I fancy myself among the pleasures of Rome!"

Nevertheless, he continued his studies. He gathered books about him. He called to him a company of pupils who served him as amanuenses. He began to learn Hebrew, a knowledge in which he differed from almost all of his Christian contemporaries. He wrote a life of Paul the Hermit, which presently took its place in the literature of the day with the Life of Antony by Athanasius, and the Life of Martin by Sulpicius. In their old age, he says, when Paul was a hundred and thirteen and Antony was ninety, the younger hermit visited the elder; and that day a raven, which for many years had brought Paul every morning half a loaf of bread, flew gently down and laid a whole loaf before them. The two saints talked together. "Tell me," said Paul, "how fares the human race? Are new homes springing up in the ancient cities? What government directs the world?" Antony knew hardly more about it than Paul himself. When Paul died, leaving as his sole possession the tunic which he had woven out of palm-leaves, two lions dug his grave. The lion which appears with Jerome in the familiar pictures is a symbol of this desert life. It came to him one day holding up a wounded paw, out of which the saint extracted a thorn.

"I beseech you, reader,"—so the Life of Paul ends,—"I beseech you, whoever you may be, to remember Jerome the sinner. He, if God would give him his choice, would much sooner take Paul's tunic with his merits, than the purple of kings with their punishments."

The troubles of the contending church followed the scholar even into the wilderness. The strife for succession to the bishopric of Antioch, which engaged the attention of the Council of Constantinople under the presidency of Gregory of Nazianzus, divided the monks, and Jerome found his peace perturbed by their debates. He went to Constantinople where he studied for a time with Gregory, and translated some of the homilies of Origen. Thence he removed to Rome, where he entered into the service of Pope Damasus. The Pope proposed questions, mostly on the interpretation of Scripture, to which Jerome wrote learned and elaborate answers. Here he continued his study of Origen, whom he followed in the collation of versions of the Septuagint, endeavoring to establish an accurate text. Here he made the translation of the Psalms into Latin which was used in the services of the Western Church for eleven centuries.

Jerome found the Roman world as he remembered it from the days of his youth. It was worse rather than better, being given over to luxury and pride and pleasure. The rich were idle, cruel and sensual. Women vied with each other in the costly splendor of their dress. Their lips were red with rouge, their faces white with gypsum, their eye-brows black with antimony. But among them were good women. The Lady Marcella, who lived in a great house on the Aventine Hill, remembered how Athanasius visited Rome, bringing with him two monks from the valley of the Nile. They had mightily impressed her in her childhood. In her house Jerome had a Bible class of wives and daughters of the Roman aristocracy. Under his instruction they studied even Hebrew. They made him their spiritual director, the keeper of their conscience. He initiated them into the discipline of the ascetic life. The Lady Paula came, a great person in the social world, and brought her daughters Blesilla and Eustochium. Jerome's influence was felt throughout the society of Rome.

The new asceticism made immediate enemies. It was opposed instinctively by all who loved the pleasures of the world. It was opposed also by those who found in its extremes a defiance of the revelation of the will of God in human nature.

Helvidius attacked its insistence on the supreme sacredness of the unmarried life. He denied the doctrine, cardinal to all ascetics, of the perpetual virginity of the mother of our Lord. The brothers and sisters, he said, of whom mention is made in the Gospels, were her children. Jerome vehemently denied this. He maintained that holiness and the normal wedded state are antagonistic. Marriage means crying children, and clamoring servants, and cooks and seamstresses, and anxiety about expense. The master comes home to dinner: the wife flutters like a swallow all about the house to see that everything is in order, and the meal ready to be served. "Tell me, I pray, where in all this is any thought of God?"

Jovinian had made trial of the ascetic life and had abandoned it. He had lived on bread and water, saying his prayers; but he had changed his mind. He had come to perceive that the laws of nature are the laws of God, and that the normal human life is acceptable with Him. In this spirit he had written books in which he declared that "virginity, widowhood and marriage are themselves indifferent, being each alike pleasing to God," and that "fasting and the thankful enjoyment of food are of equal moral validity." To these propositions, which to us are common-places of religion, Jerome opposed himself with the fierceness of a garrison whose strong tower is beset by the enemy. He went so far as to denounce marriage as a state of sin, and so scandalized sober persons by his destructive enthusiasm that Augustine had to write a treatise on the Good of Marriage to counteract his teaching. Jerome himself withdrew the more extreme statements of his position, and in a letter to a friend excused himself by the significant statement that "it is one thing to argue, and another thing to teach." Anything, he held, is fair in the battle of debate.

Vigilantius, like Jovinian, saw the increasing perils of asceticism. He felt that the life of religion was being corrupted by superstitious devotions, especially the new honors which were being paid to the relics of the saints. He had the courage to oppose the whole current of the Christian life as Jerome directed it, declaring that paganism and polytheism were being invited back into the church. Jerome in reply called him Dormitantius, and said that he was talking in his sleep, and snoring instead of arguing. He wished that he could deal with him as the blessed Paul dealt with Ananias and Sapphira.

Jerome arraigned the whole world, lay and clerical. In an amazing letter to Eustochium he advised her as to her companions. She must avoid the society of married women, especially those of rank and wealth, who wear robes inwrought with threads of gold. She must have no intercourse with widows, who go abroad in capacious litters, with red cloaks, looking for new husbands. "Let your companions be women pale and thin with fasting." She must shun all men, especially clergymen, and more particularly such clergymen as "use perfumes freely, and see that there are no creases in their shoes. Their curling hair shows traces of the tongs; their fingers glisten with rings; they walk on tiptoe across a damp road, not to splash their feet."

The letter is of much interest to the student of Roman manners in the fourth century, but it is easy to see how the publication of it increased the hostility which was rising against the plain-speaking monk who wrote it. The young men of Rome already hated the man who told the young women not to marry. The clergy hated him whose austere life was a criticism upon their comfortable ways. When presently Blesilla died, and the rumor went abroad that she had been killed by the monastic discipline to which she had subjected herself, there was a riot at her funeral, and people cried, "The monks to the Tiber!" Then Pope Damasus came to the end of his days, and in his death Jerome lost his strong protector. He had to leave the city. He betook himself to Bethlehem, whither Paula and Eustochium followed him.

On the eve of his departure Jerome wrote a letter to the Lady Asella, defending himself against the slanders of the city. They call me, he said, an infamous person, crafty and slippery and a liar. At first they said that I was holy and humble and eloquent, and that I ought to be a bishop. Now the place is filled with gossip about me and the holy Paula, "one who mourns and fasts, who is squalid with neglect, and almost blind with weeping, whose delights are self-denials, and whose life a fast." "I thank my God that I am worthy of the hatred of the world."

Friends and disciples accompanied the pilgrims, and in Bethlehem they built monasteries, with Paula's money. She presided over one, ruling a community of holy women; he presided over the other. And they maintained together a guest-house for travellers, so that if Joseph and Mary came that way again there should be hospitality for them at the inn.

Jerome was now forty-one years old, and had thirty-four years yet to live. He devoted himself to his interrupted studies. He opened a school for the Bethlehem children, teaching them Greek and Latin. He took up again the study of Hebrew. Every day Paula and Eustochium came over to the pleasant cave which he called the "paradise of studies" and together they read the Bible and discoursed upon it. There it was that Postumianus found him, "always at his books with his whole heart." There he kept the discipline of the monastic life, wearing the brown habit of a hermit, and sweetening all his studies with his prayers.

He never succeeded in sweetening his temper. His wrath still broke out as of old against his critics and his enemies, and against all heretics. He set an example which poisoned the whole stream of controversy down to very recent times. Nothing was too bad for him to say about those with whom he disagreed. But he appreciated the peace of Bethlehem. "Here bread, and herbs grown with our own hands, and milk, rural delicacies, afford us humble but wholesome food. Living thus, sleep does not overtake us in prayer, satiety does not interfere with study. In summer, the trees afford us shade. In autumn, the air is cool, and the fallen leaves give us a quiet resting-place. In spring the field is clothed with flowers, and we sing our songs the sweeter among the singing of the birds. When the winter is cold, and the snow comes, we have no lack of wood, and I watch or sleep warm enough. Let Rome keep its crowds, let its arena be cruel, its circus go wild, its theatre indulge in luxury, and—not to forget our friends—let the senate of ladies exchange their daily visits. Our happiness is to cleave to the Lord, and to put our trust in the Lord God." It is a pleasant picture, in happy contrast with the barren deserts in which Paul and Antony lived their painful lives.

The chief fruit of these years of quiet and congenial study was the Latin translation of the Bible, called the Vulgate.

The Psalter, which Jerome had published in Rome, was translated from the Septuagint, and kept its place in the service of the church in spite of the Psalter which he now translated from the Hebrew; as the Psalms of Coverdale remain to-day in the Book of Common Prayer, in spite of the new translations of 1611 and 1885. But the rest of Jerome's Bible superseded all existing versions. Throughout the Middle Ages all European Christendom read the Scriptures in the words which he had written. For a great part of the Western Church, his translation is the Bible to this day. The men who made the English Bible which we use had Jerome's sentences by heart, and the cadences of them still sound in the sacred pages which we read and in the prayers which we pray.

Toxotius, the son of Paula, and representative of her great Roman house, married the daughter of Albinus who in his day was Pontifex Maximus in the persisting paganism in which he lived and died. But their little daughter Paula was baptized a Christian. Jerome in his last years, advised that the letters of the alphabet be written on separate pieces of ivory for the child to play with, that she might thus begin her education. A pleasant legend, celebrated in Domenichino's famous picture, said that the last sacrament was administered to Jerome by the hand of St. Augustine.

CHAPTER X

AUGUSTINE

In the congregation of St. Ambrose at Milan, in the latter part of the fourth century, there was a young man with whom many persons are better acquainted than with some of their intimate friends. He wrote an account of his life, in which he set down with exceeding frankness not only what he had done, but what he had thought. And this account remains to this day. It is the earliest of autobiographies. Here, for the first time since the world began, did a man write a book about himself. Even now, after these fifteen hundred years, it is still the best of such books.

Benvenuto Cellini gave an interesting and entertaining account of himself, telling honestly how faithfully he prayed and how frequently he broke the Ten Commandments, and thereby revealing the mediaeval conscience. John Bunyan, in "Grace Abounding," recounted his religious experience, with a statement of his faults so frank that it went beyond the fact, and revealed thereby the self-accusing conscience of the Puritan. But the supreme autobiography is the "Confessions" of St. Augustine.

The book had no precedent, and in its form it has had no imitator; for it is in the form of prayer,— the longest printed prayer. From beginning to end, the writer addresses himself to God. To read it is to over-hear a penitent at his devotions.

I

The Making of a Saint: The *Confessions*

Augustine was born in the middle of the fourth century, in the Roman province of Africa, in Tagaste, a country town of Numidia. Of the two great Christian fathers of that neighborhood, Cyprian had been dead a hundred years, and Tertullian a hundred and fifty; but they were remembered as Whitefield and Edwards are remembered in New England. In spite of these devout memories Carthage was still a pagan city. Augustine's mother was a Christian, but his father was a pagan.

A recent writer, in a book upon which a very re-spectable English publisher put his imprint, cast it up as a reproach against the Christian Church that its theology for a thousand years was dominated by a black man. The idea was that all people who lived in Africa must be of African descent. A similar course of reasoning would include to-day the English governors of Egypt. Augustine's name is evidence of his Roman ancestry. His people came from Italy.

Monica, the mother of Augustine, belongs to the shining company of saintly wives and mothers who have contended successfully with difficult domestic conditions. For many years, neither her husband nor her son showed any interest in religion, and during much of that time they lived not only irreligious but immoral lives. The attainment of her prayers in the final conversion of them both has ever since been an inspiration to maternal faith and patience.

As for Augustine's father, the only thing which is set down to his credit is the fact that he did not beat his wife. The discipline of wives was a part of the common life of the time. Almost all of the friends of Monica appeared occasionally with bruised faces. Her immunity was a continual perplexity to the neighborhood. She explained that it takes two to make a quarrel.

Augustine learned to pray at his mother's knee, but he was not baptized. The age of thirty was considered the proper time for baptism, following the example of Christ. The life of Augustine represents a transition in the doctrine of baptism from one superstition to another. In his infancy the idea was that the water of baptism washed away all sin; it was well to defer the cleansing bath till the temptations of youth were past. In his maturity the idea was that without baptism salvation was impossible, or at the least uncertain; infants must be baptized in order to be saved.

He went to church with his mother in his early childhood, but soon showed a disposition to follow the example of his father. He says that he was a bad boy at school, neglecting his studies, running away to play ball, in spite of his mother's diligent beating. He liked Latin, but hated Greek much, and mathematics more.

Going to college in Carthage, he changed from bad to worse. He made the acquaintance of evil companions, and exposed himself to all the temptations of the college and the city. This, he says, was not wholly from a love of wrong, but in great part from a love of praise. He desired admiration, and tried to get it by making himself out worse than he was, and boasting of misdemeanors which he never did. A common prank of college life in Carthage was to break up lectures by disturbances in class rooms. A gang of youths would go about from room to room for the purpose of annoying the instructors. Augustine either belonged to such a crowd or sympathized with their performances. These, however, were minor offences. Carthage was still the same hard town against which the soul of Tertullian had revolted. Augustine entered into its vicious ways. At the age of eighteen, he took a wife, without the observance of any formality either civil or ecclesiastical. He seemed to be going to the devil.

In this darkness, there were two rays of light. One was the fact that the boy, with all his disregard of study, had a singularly able mind. The other was the fact that he was dissatisfied and unhappy. He says that he was as one who has lost his way, and earnestly desires to get out of the woods into the road, but knows not in what direction to turn. The note of this whole period of his life is in the first paragraph of the "Confessions": "Thou, O God, hast made us for Thyself, and our hearts are restless till they find rest in Thee."

He was recalled in some measure from his evil courses by reading a book of Cicero, the "Hortensius," now lost. It stirred in him the spirit of speculation and of aspiration. That the lad of nineteen was interested in such a book shows that he was different from his companions. Cicero had much to say about the quest of truth. He exalted truth for its own sake, apart from all entanglements of formularies, as the most precious of possessions. He taught also that truth is to be attained by the pure mind, along the way of character.

In order to get strength to realize this ideal Augustine associated himself with the Manichæans. They attracted him as the Montanists had attracted Tertullian.

Manichæism was a new religion which had been founded in the middle of the third century by Mani, a Persian prophet. He appeared as a man of God, having a message from on high. At first he proclaimed his revelation with acceptance, but presently opposition arose from the established religion of Zoroaster, and the prophet was crucified. Thereupon his doctrines were carried east and west, east to India and China, west to Italy and Africa.

The basis of Manichæism was the dualistic theology of Zoroaster. There are two gods, good and bad, corresponding to the two sides of human life, symbolized by day and night, by joy and sorrow, by life and death. The son of the good god invaded the kingdom of the bad god and was taken captive. His father came and rescued him, but in the struggle he lost a great treasure of celestial light. To keep this treasure from recovery by the good god, the bad god placed it in man who was created for that purpose,—a little light in every man. Here are we, then, children of the devil, but having within us a celestial spark. The problem of human life is how to free this bit of heaven from the bondage of matter. To aid in this endeavor came first the prophets, then Jesus Christ, then the Holy Spirit whose coming Christ foretold, and who was present in the world in the person of Mani. Man proceeds along the way of life according to counsels and directions which are given him as he advances from grade to grade of the Manichæan mysteries. At last he attains to life eternal. Into this system of religion, the Manichæans brought occult doctrines of stars, and dealt in magic, and cast horoscopes.

Manichæism attracted Augustine by its appeal to his intelligence. It offered a solution of the problem of evil. It gave a rational explanation of sin and pain. It showed how a bad world and a good God could exist together. And this explanation was in accord with the current philosophy, according to which matter is essentially evil, and the source of evil. To this was added an exhilarating sense of freedom, an intellectual liberty, a large license of criticism of the past. For Mani proposed his religion as an advance beyond Judaism and Christianity, and his followers felt privileged to read both Testaments with discrimination, choosing here, and refusing there.

Manichæism further attracted Augustine by its appeal to his conscience. It convicted him of sin. It set before him a conception of the wickedness of the world which was in accordance with his own experience, and offered him a way out. It proposed a plan of salvation. It did not disclose the details of this plan. These were reserved to be communicated to the disciple little by little, as he passed from grade to grade. This reservation was in itself attractive by reason of the element of mystery. It encouraged and maintained devout expectation. The disciple began as a "hearer," serving a long novitiate; then he became an "adept"; and there were attainments of degrees beyond that. Augustine never advanced beyond the preparatory stage, but the undisclosed central sanctuary gave significance to all the approaches, however distant. He hoped to escape at last from sin, and find peace and blessing. Meanwhile, the doctrine that the struggle of which he was conscious in his own soul was part of a vast universal contention between rival gods gave new dignity to his life.

By this time Augustine had completed his college course, and had returned to his native town as a teacher of rhetoric, or, as we would say, literature. He read the Latin classics with his students. But the sudden death of a young man to whom he was devotedly attached so saddened him that he felt impelled to leave the scenes of a friendship so tragically interrupted. He returned to Carthage, and began to lecture. He now found that the custom of disturbing lecture-rooms, which had been so pleasant to him as a student, was by no means so agreeable from his point of view as teacher. Augustine disliked it so much that he left Carthage and went to Rome. But the Roman students had a way of their own quite as inconvenient as the boisterous manners of the Carthaginians. They were much more courteous in their behavior, but they evaded the payment of their bills. When the end of the course approached, and pay-day with it, they absented themselves, and the teacher found himself without support. Happily, at this moment there was a vacancy in the professorship of rhetoric at Milan. This was a government position, and the salary was paid by the state. Augustine applied for the position. The prefect Symmachus approved, and he was appointed. To Milan, then, he went, taking with him his mother, his wife, his little son Adeodatus, and Alypius, a friend.

Being thus established at Milan, Augustine rejected Manichæism. This he did in part because he lost faith in the veracity of horoscopes; a slave and a prince might be born under the same star: but also because he observed that the practice of some eminent Manichæans contradicted their professions.

He was now reading Aristotle, and that master's emphasis on facts, demanding a solid basis of reality, completed his conversion from a religion whose theology was mainly constructed out of imagination. Indeed, the clear intellect of Aristotle served for a time to turn Augustine from all creeds, and all faith in whatever could not be proved by processes of reason. Again he drifted without anchor, blown by the shifting winds.

Out of this condition, Neoplatonism came to save him. In the doctrines of this philosophy, subordinating all things material, finding all reality in God, and all worthy occupation in the endeavor to know God and to be in communion with Him, Augustine found nourishment for the mystical side of his nature.

It is a curious fact that at this moment, as he was committing himself to a career which demanded first purgation, then illumination, then separation from the world, Augustine looked about with deliberate prudence for a rich wife. He had proposed to establish a little community of philosophers, wherein he and a few congenial companions might debate without interruption the problems of the soul. But such a community must have a financial basis. Even after the plan failed, Augustine found that his creditors interrupted the serenity of his thought. So he proposed to improve his condition by marrying money. A young woman was found who on her side was willing to undertake the perilous adventure of marrying philosophy. They were accordingly betrothed. Thereupon Augustine discarded his true wife, the mother of his son, who had lived with him faithfully for thirteen years. She was his wife, saving only the formulas of church and state. But he put her away, keeping his son, sending her back to Africa. And to these transactions, the good Monica gave her approval.

We are following the frank story of the "Confessions," saying to ourselves, How contemporary it all is! and of a sudden we come on such an incident as this, and we perceive that after all we are dealing with a Roman African, in the end of the fourth century. Happily, the conversion of Augustine to the Christian religion put a stop to all further matrimonial progress. The young girl with the great fortune passes out of sight between the lines of the book and is heard of no more.

Meanwhile, Augustine had been attending the services of the church in Milan. Ambrose had strongly appealed to him, a great noble who had become a great bishop. He heard him often. He perceived that Ambrose was basing truth on authority, telling the people that they ought to believe thus and so because that was the doctrine of the church.

This teaching was the result of Ambrose's own experience. Coming to his place as bishop straight from civil life, having never so much as opened a book of theology before the day of his ordination, and being so busy from that time forward that serious study was almost impossible, he had been obliged to take the doctrines of divinity at second hand. And to this his administrative genius further inclined him. He regarded the church from the point of view of an experienced state official. He saw the working advantage of a general uniformity of thought and action: men must do as they are told, and believe as they are taught. This was the attitude not of Ambrose only, but of the West in general. It was characteristic of the Occidental mind, impatient of metaphysics, caring for conduct rather than for creed. To Augustine, after his fruitless wanderings, seeking truth and finding no abiding satisfaction, the position of Ambrose was appealingly attractive. Tossed by waves and buffeted by winds, he was invited into the secure harbor of the church.

Then on a day when Augustine with a group of friends was discussing the problems of the religious life, one told the story of St. Antony as written by St. Athanasius: how for love of Christ he had abandoned all and followed Him. The recital impressed Augustine profoundly. He listened with tears. Disturbed in mind, restless, dissatisfied, reproached by his conscience, called of God but returning no reply, he parted from his companions, and going into a little quiet garden behind the house began to consider his forlorn condition. "How long," he lamented to himself, "shall I be as one who wakes in the morning and knows that he should rise, but rises not? How long shall I pray, O God, make me a Christian—but not yet!"

Suddenly he heard a voice as of a child, singing over and over as if it were the refrain of a song, "Take and read! Take and read! Take and read!" He received the words as a message from on high. He understood them to have reference to the Bible. That book he was to take and read. He took the book, and let it fall open where it would, and read, "Let us walk honestly, as in the day; not in rioting and drunkenness, not in chambering and wantonness, not in strife and envying. But put ye on the Lord Jesus Christ, and make not provision for the flesh, to fulfill the lusts thereof." "Instantly," he says, "as if the light of salvation had been poured into my heart with the close of the sentence, all the darkness of my doubts had fled away."

Nothing so important in the history of Christianity had happened since the heavens opened over the road to Damascus. The dominance of Augustine in Western theology can be compared only to the universal dominance of Paul. He directed the thought not only of the Middle Ages, but of the Reformation.

Immediately, Augustine informed Ambrose of his desire to be baptized, and retired with a few friends into the country to prepare himself. There they exercised their bodies in the fields, and their minds in long debates on the Blessed Life, the Order of Providence, and kindred themes in religion and philosophy. Then on Easter Even, 387, Augustine was made a member of the Christian Church.

There is no foundation for the tradition that the Te Deum was composed on that occasion, Augustine and Ambrose singing the great words in turn. That hymn was composed about that time, but probably by Nicetas, a missionary bishop in Dacia. It expresses, however, the faith and praise with which their hearts were filled.

Augustine resigned his professorship to devote himself entirely to the service of religion. He determined to return to his own land. One evening at the port of Ostia, where they waited for the ship which was to carry them to Africa, Augustine and his mother sat together in the moonlight, looking out over the sea, talking long and intimately of the past and the future, and especially of the religion which had transformed his life. There they sat as Ary Scheffer represents them in his famous picture. And Monica said, "My son, I am now altogether satisfied. Why should I live longer? The hopes and prayers of all my life are answered."

The next day she fell sick, and in a little while she died.

With the death of Monica the autobiographical part of the "Confessions" ends. Augustine wrote the book twelve years after, in order, as he said, to show out of how deep a depth a soul may cry to God and be answered and delivered. Of all the writing of the early church this is the only book which is known to-day to the untechnical reader, the only contribution of the time to the common treasury of literature.

The interests of men change, their emphasis passes from one matter to another, even the theology of the old time becomes unreadable to the new generations; but human nature remains the same. It is forever contemporary. The "Confessions" is one of the immortal books, with the epics of Homer and the dialogues of Plato, because it is an honest disclosure of the temptations, the contentions, the aspirations of the soul of man.

II

The Bishop of Hippo

The return of Augustine to Africa marks the beginning of the second of the two major divisions of his life. Out of his novitiate he passed into his ministry.

He spent three years in monastic seclusion, though not in solitude. He kept a group of friends about him. They lived on the farm which had been the property of his father. There they set the example in Africa of that spiritual discipline which Basil and Gregory had practised in the East, and Martin and Cassian and Jerome had preached in the West.

After three years of this delightful quiet, being on a Sunday in the neighboring town of Hippo, the bishop of that place in his sermon reminded the congregation that he was growing old and feeble, and that being himself a Greek it was particularly hard for him to preach in Latin. The people, understanding what was in his mind, seized upon Augustine whose holy life they knew, and demanded that he become the bishop's assistant. To this he reluctantly consented. He was ordained, and entered upon his duties. By and by, the bishop died, and Augustine became bishop of Hippo in his place. There he continued forty years, all the remainder of his life.

Hippo is still a populated place, in Algiers, two hundred miles west of Tunis. The neighborhood is singularly suitable for the observation of eclipses of the sun, and thereby invites the visits of both English and American astronomers. An aqueduct of the time of Hadrian remains from the town which Augustine knew. The city in his day had a wall about it, and its inhabitants were sixty thousand. The great Basilica, his cathedral, stood on high ground in the midst of the city, among almond and orange trees, looking towards the sea and the far hills of Tunis. In 1890, Cardinal Lavigerie consecrated a new cathedral on the site of the old, naming it in memory of him who is still spoken of, even by the Mohammedan inhabitants, as the Great Christian.

There Augustine went about his business as a bishop. In all simplicity, without ostentation, in a day when bishops lived like princes, he ministered to the fishermen of Hippo. With much strictness of personal

241

abstinence, he maintained a modest hospitality. A sentence carved on the table in his dining-room reminded his guests that as for those who were disposed to speak unfriendly of their neighbors, their room was better than their company. He gathered his clergy about him, to live under his own roof. He required them to follow that ascetic life in which he set them an example. He forbade them to have private property, or to be married. He set forth for their guidance a rule of life, adapted to those who having their daily occupation in the world were intent on the improvement of their souls. In the eleventh century, this rule, or what was thought to be this rule, was adopted by the clerical order of Augustinians, the Austin Canons, in whose house at Erfurt Martin Luther studied the Bible and prepared himself to undertake the German Reformation.

In the midst of these quiet labors came three determining events: two controversies and a great calamity.

The controversies, one with the Donatists, the other with the Pelagians, were characteristic of the Christianity of the West. The Western Church had regarded the Arian Debate with perplexity and impatience. The discussion had been carried on in Greek, a language with which the West was imperfectly acquainted. The General Council at Nicæa under Constantine, which proclaimed the Nicene faith, and the General Council at Constantinople under Theodosius, which confirmed it, had been remote from the concerns of Europe. There were but seven Western bishops at Nicæa, and none at all at Constantinople.

Moreover, the theme of the debate had been foreign to the active and practical interests of the Western mind. The Eastern bishops of eminence were for the most part theologians, of a speculative habit of thought; the eminent bishops of the West were for the most part ecclesiastics, administrative persons. Thus while the Eastern Church was vexed with heresies, arising from differences in theology, the Western Church was vexed with schisms, arising from differences concerning organization. And when a notable heresy did appear in the West,—the Pelagian,—it was concerned not with the nature of God, but with the nature of man: it had to do with practical human life.

Against the erection of a complete and exclusive organization, the Donatists had long since protested. They had now been a separate church for nearly two hundred years. They were especially strong in Africa. There were Donatist churches side by side with the Catholic churches in Hippo. So intimate was the contention that no Donatist woman would bake a loaf of bread for a Catholic. And there was frequent violence.

Augustine at first addressed himself to the reconciliation of this inveterate division. But the original arguments for and against were now so entangled with prejudices, so complicated by years of abusive controversy, and so lost under an increasing burden of fresh grievances, that no friendly settlement seemed possible. The cruelties of imperial soldiers against the Donatists had been answered with fierce reprisals. In Augustine's own time and neighborhood, one Catholic bishop had been ducked in a pond, and another had been beaten about the head with the pieces of his broken altar. Augustine himself was in frequent peril.

In his books against the Donatists, Augustine shows the effects of this contention. First of all great Christian teachers, he formally defended the persecution of heretics. The shedding of the blood of the Priscillianists had indeed been undertaken at the instigation of bishops, but other and better bishops had deplored it. Here, however, were heretics destroying churches and assaulting clergy. Their evil must be met with evil. Their violence must be resisted with violence. Augustine tried in vain to keep the precepts of the Sermon on the Mount. He was disposed to love his enemies. But he hated the Donatists. They seemed to him to be outside the limits of Christian forbearance. He advised treating them as thieves and robbers should be treated. In a writing entitled "De Correctione Donatistanum," he held that the civil power ought to restrain schism. He was the first to translate the hospitality of a parable into the hostility of a religious war, and to find a sanction for persecution in the words "Compel them to come in." He might as well have taken for a text, "Rise, Peter, kill and eat!" The principle proceeded easily from the punishment of wrong acting to the punishment of wrong thinking. Augustine became an apostle of intolerance. Thus the controversy with the Donatists continued until all the clamorous voices were silenced, in the year when Augustine died, by the victorious invasion of the Vandals.

The heresy of the Pelagians turned upon the question, How may we be saved from sin? An answer was given by a Briton, named Pelagius. He said, "We may be saved by being good." He quoted the words of Jesus, "If thou wilt enter into life, keep the commandments." Anybody, he said, can do that, if he tries hard enough. The church is not necessary, the sacraments are not necessary, the grace of God is not necessary. These are all helpful, but not essential. Be good: this is the desire of God, and it is possible to every child of God.

The matter became a subject of controversy in connection with the letters of congratulation which were written to Demetrias, a young Roman lady who had entered the monastic life. Jerome said that this was the most important event in the history of Rome since the defeat of Hannibal. But Pelagius was not so enthusiastic. He acknowledged the excellences of the single life, but observed that there was danger of overestimating them. Men and women could be holy, if they would, under any conditions. The natural life was as acceptable to God as the ascetic life. He praised the innate goodness of human nature, and protested against the theory that man's will is totally corrupt.

The letter precipitated a general discussion, and Pelagius, a sweet-tempered, simple-hearted person, who in his own experience and observation had encountered much more good than ill, found that he had drawn upon himself the fire of the great guns of Augustine.

Never has the personal equation entered more evidently into the progress of thought. To Augustine, with his hot African nature, remembering his own participation in the wickedness of the world, the supreme fact of human life is sin. Taking his clue from expressions of St. Paul, he traced it back to the first man. The spring of humanity was poisoned at its source. Every human being is born bad. The race is lost, and every member of it, by nature inclined to evil, is not only unable to do good, but is doomed, in consequence of this inability, to everlasting punishment.

Accordingly, salvation cannot come by any effort of our own. It must be derived from without. In his teaching as to the source of salvation, Augustine presented his two characteristic doctrines.

The first doctrine was that salvation comes by grace. Grace is help from God. To a part—a small part—of our doomed race, by reason of the act of His inscrutable will, God gives grace, and they are saved. The sacrifice of Christ upon the cross makes grace available, but it becomes applicable to us not by any act of ours, not of ourselves. The saved were chosen of God, elect, predestinated to eternal life, before the world began.

The second doctrine was that grace comes by the church. It cannot be had outside the church. It is a subtle something which is imparted by the sacraments. Outside the church, then, among the schismatics, among the Donatists, is no salvation. All the heathen are lost. Infants dying unbaptized are not saved; they may be punished with some measure of mercy, and be damned with a somewhat mitigated damnation, but they cannot enter into heaven. The church is in the world as the ark floated on the flood. Unless we get in and stay in, we shall certainly be drowned in an ocean of everlasting fire.

The Pelagians said that Augustine's doctrines were immoral. If man has no free will, then he has no responsibility, and there is no difference between vice and virtue. They said that Augustine's doctrines were blasphemous. The condemnation of a race for the sins of one would be a horrible injustice, not to be attributed to God. They said that Augustine had been a Manichee, and had believed in a bad god, and had never been converted. But the church went with Augustine. In the breaking-up of the Roman Empire by the invasion of the barbarians, in the violence and misery of the time, in the prevalence of evil, in the face of the wicked world, he seemed a true interpreter of human life.

Toward the end of his long career Augustine did a curious and interesting thing. He published a good-sized book called "Retractations." In it he confessed the errors of his teaching. Concerning this matter and that he had changed his mind, in the better light of experience and truth. It was characteristic of his habitual humility and honesty. He did not retract, however, the positions which he took against the Donatists and the Pelagians. By virtue of these positions, he was the founder of Latin Christianity.

At last, in the midst of these controversies, came the great calamity of the fall of Rome.

Gradually, step by step, the barbarians had passed over the boundaries of the Danube and the Rhine into the empire. Constantine had held them in check, but after him they came in greater might than ever. They presented themselves as settlers, and were received as allies. These two aspects of their invasion dimmed the sight of the Romans regarding the tremendous changes which were taking place. Theodosius mastered them as long as his strong reign continued. After him his son Honorius reigned with incredible indifference in the West, and the barbarian Stilicho became his minister of state. And after Stilicho came Alaric.

Jerome writes in 409: "Innumerable savage tribes have overrun all parts of Gaul. The whole country between the Alps and the Pyrenees, between the Rhine and the ocean, has been laid waste by Quadi, Vandals, Sarmatians, Alans, Gepidi, Herules, Saxons, Burgundians, Allemans and, alas for the common weal, even the hordes of the Pannonians. The once noble city of Mainz has been captured and destroyed. In its church many thousands have been massacred. The people of Worms have been extirpated after a long siege. The powerful city of Rheims, the Ambiani [near Amiens], the Altrabtae [near Arras], the Belgians on the outskirts of the world, Tournay, Speyer and Strassburg have fallen to the Germans. The provinces of Aquitaine, and of the Nine Nations, of Lyons and Narbonne, with the exception of a few cities, have been laid waste. Those whom the sword spares without, famine ravages within. I cannot speak of Toulouse without tears. I am silent about other places, that I may not seem to despair of God's mercy."

In 410 Alaric the Goth besieged Rome and took it. The eternal city, the immemorial metropolis of the world, the invincible and inviolable fortress of civilization, fell and was plundered by the Goths.

By the emperor Honorius, in his court at Ravenna, the news was received with that amazing indifference which was his most marked characteristic. He is said to have shown in his career only two signs of any interest in life: he had a strong sense of the importance of keeping his imperial person out of danger, and he had remarkable success in raising hens. Messengers brought the emperor the awful news. "Rome," they cried, "is destroyed!" "What!" he said, "only this morning she was feeding out of my hand"; and when they made him understand that it was the imperial city of which they spoke, he replied, greatly relieved, "Oh, I thought you meant my favorite hen, of the same name!"

But to Jerome at Bethlehem, Augustine at Hippo, and all other thoughtful Romans, it seemed to be, as indeed it was, the end of the age.

Then Augustine wrote his greatest work, the "City of God." The purpose was to show that though the city of the world had fallen, the City of God stands strong forever. This writing is in twenty-two books. Ten are negative, showing the falsity of paganism: five to disprove that the present prosperity of man is dependent on the pagan gods; five to deny that they have anything to do with man's prosperity hereafter. Even in the fifth century, two hundred years after the conversion of Constantine, paganism was still of sufficient importance to call for this long and laborious refutation. The other twelve books are positive, setting forth the truth of the Christian religion: four about its origin, four about its growth, four to set in contrast the cities of the world secular and temporal, and the church, the city of the world spiritual and eternal.

With this work, the Early Church, and the Roman world with it, spoke its last word. After that, amidst the confusions and distresses of the barbarian invasion of the empire, the learning and literature of the time lapsed, for the most part, into the making of copies and compilations of previous opinions. Augustine's "City of God" served as a treasure house of theological material throughout the Middle Ages. It was a store of thought by which men lived in times of intellectual famine.

In 429, the Vandals under Genseric invaded Africa. Down they came over "the shining fields which had been the granary of Rome." In the common destruction of the country, the force of the invasion fell terribly upon the churches. When the Vandals came, Africa had five hundred bishops; twenty years after only eighteen dioceses had survived.

The invaders besieged Hippo. Augustine was in his seventy-fifth year. In the third month of the siege (430) he fell into a mortal sickness. The last of the fathers, the last of the great Romans, lay dying, as the empire, wounded beyond recovery, lay dying beside him. Outside the sickroom was the noise of fighting, and the shouts of the besiegers. Thus the city of his long service faded from Augustine's eyes, and he entered into that other city of which he wrote, the city of his hopes and prayers, the divine city, founded, as he said, on earth, but eternal in the heavens.

APPENDIX

TABLES OF DATES

I

THE ROMAN EMPERORS FROM AUGUSTUS TO AUGUSTULUS

The Pagan Empire

I

B.C.
  27. Augustus.

A.D.
  14. Tiberius.
  37. Gaius.
  41. Claudius.
  54. Nero.
  68,69. Galba, Otho, Vitellius.
  69. Vespasian.
  79. Titus.
  81. Domitian.
  96. Nerva.
  98. Trajan.

II

117. Hadrian.
138. Antoninus Pius.
161. Marcus Aurelius.
180. Commodus.
193. Septimius Severus.

III

211. Caracalla.
218. Elagabalus.
222. Alexander Severus.
235. Maximinus.
238. Gordian.
244. Philip.
249. Decius.
251. Gallus.
253. Valerian.
270. Aurelian.
284. Diocletian, with Maximian.
305. Constantius and Galerius.
311. Constantine and Licinius.

The Christian Empire

324. Constantine.
337. Constantine II, Constantius II, Constans.
350. Constantius II.
361. Julian.
363. Jovian.

West		*East*
364. Valentinian I.		364. Valens.
375. Gratian and	.	379. Theodosius I.
Valentinian II.		
383. Valentinian II.		

392. Theodosius I.

West	East
395. Honorius.	395. Arcadius.
423. Valentinian III.	408. Theodosius II.
455. Maximus.	450. Marcian.
455. Avitus.	
457. Majorian.	457. Leo I.
461. Severus.	
467. Anthemius.	
472. Olybrius.	
473. Glycerius.	
474. Julius Nepos.	474. Leo II.
475. Romulus Augustulus.	

II

THE PERSECUTIONS, FROM THE FIRE IN ROME TO THE EDICT OF MILAN

Local Persecutions

Under Nero,   64.

Under Domitian,   95.

In Bithynia (Pliny and Trajan), about   113.

Martyrdom of Ignatius,   117.

Martyrdom of Polycarp,   155.

Martyrs of Lyons,   177.

Scillitan Martyrs,   180.

Martyrs of Carthage (Perpetua, Felicitas),   202.

General Persecutions

After more than forty years of peace the First General Persecution under Decius, 249–251, under Valerian, 258–260: ten years.

After more than forty years of peace again, the Second General Persecution, under Diocletian and Galerius, 303–311: ten years.

Edict of Milan (decreeing toleration), 313.

III

THE ADVANCE OF THE BARBARIANS

Marcomanni and Quadi cross the Danube, overrun Pannonia, and are driven back by Marcus Aurelius, 174.

Alamanni and Franks cross the Rhine, 286.

Goths cross the Danube, overrun the Balkans, defeat and kill Decius, 251. In the reign of Gallienus, 260–268, they raid Asia Minor; they sack Athens, Corinth and Sparta.

Dacia is abandoned by Aurelian, 270-275.

Alamanni and Franks driven back by Probus, 276, by Constantine, 306–312, by Julian, 356–360, and by Valentinian I, 364–375.

Picts and Scots attack Britain from the north, 367–370, Saxons from the south.

Goths, pressed by Huns, settle south of the Danube, defeat and kill Valens, 378, and advance to Constantinople, but are conciliated by Theodosius.

Throughout fourth century, barbarians are gradually settling south of the Rhine and the Danube, enlisting in Roman armies, and gaining places of power in imperial courts. Rufinus the Goth is prime minister of Arcadius, Stilicho the Vandal is prime minister of Honorius.

Britain is abandoned early in fifth century, about 410.

Alaric the Visigoth crosses the Alps and takes Rome, 410.

Visigoths settle in Gaul; Vandals settle in Spain.

Gaiseric (Genseric) the Vandal conquers Roman Africa, 429.

Attila the Hun, ruler of northern and central Europe, invades Gaul and Italy, but is defeated at Chalons, 451.

Ricimer the Suebe rules Italy, appointing four successive emperors, 456–472.

Orestes the Pannonian makes his own son emperor under the title Romulus, called "Augustulus," 475.

Odoacer the Rugian deposes Augustulus and brings to an end the succession of Roman emperors, 476.

IV

HERETICS AND SCHISMATICS, FROM CERINTHUS TO PLAGIUS

Ebionites. Judaic-Christians, accepting the Gospel but keeping the Law also. Adding to the Law the practice of asceticism and "doctrines of angels," they were precursors of Gnosticism. Like-minded with them was Cerinthus, late in first century.

Gnostics. Matter essentially evil, God infinitely remote. God and the world connected by inferior divine beings called æons. Simon Magus in Samaria. Basilides, Valentinus (d. 160). Marcion in Rome upheld the Gospel against the Law, accounting himself a champion of St. Paul.

Docetics. The idea that matter is evil contradicted the doctrine of the incarnation: Jesus had only the appearance of a body, and of a human life.

Montanists. They expected speedy end of the world. Their prophets spoke, they said, by immediate inspiration: no need of any ordination. Opposed secularism and formalism: Montanus and Tertullian (d. 222).

Adoptionists. Jesus is God by adoption, not by incarnation. God entered into Him at baptism, departed at crucifixion.

Sabellians, Modalists, Patripassians. Father and Son and Holy Ghost are only names of God, indicating divine aspects and activities. Opponents said that the doctrine implied the suffering and death of God. Paul of Samosata (260) taught that Jesus by His unique goodness rose to divine dignity. Those who held the theory that the names Father and Son signify only two different relations of God to the world were also called *Monarchians*. The most famous teacher of this doctrine was Sabellius.

Novatians. In Rome, after Decian persecution, they held that Christians who had lapsed should not be restored to membership in the church. They formed separate societies.

Meletians. In Alexandria, after Diocletian persecution, they insisted on subjecting the lapsed to severe penance. They also formed societies outside the church.

Donatists. In Carthage, after Diocletian persecution, they refused to recognize clergy who had surrendered sacred books. Condemned at Council of Arles (314) they established churches of their own.

Arians. The Son is a divine being, existing before the beginning of the world but not from eternity, having been created by the Father. Arius of Alexandria condemned by Council of Nicæa (325). The Nicene fathers held that the Son is "of one substance" *(homoousios)* with the Father.

Homoiousians. They held that the Son is "of like substance" with the Father.

Anomæans, Eunomeans. They held that the Son is "of unlike substance" with the Father. Thus taught

Aëtius of Antioch (d. 360) and his pupil Eunomius (d. 392).

Semi-Arians, Macedonians. Named from Macedonius, bishop of Constantinople (d. 360). Orthodox as to the Son, but Arian as to the Spirit. The name is also applied to those who said "the Son is like the Father."

Apollinarians. Christ human in body and soul, but the human mind in Him was replaced by the divine mind. Condemned by Council of Constantinople (381).

Pelagians. Named from Pelagius who came from Britain to Rome early in fifth century. He upheld the freedom of the will against the doctrine of total depravity taught by Augustine. His motto was "If I ought, I can." The doctrine was condemned by Council of Ephesus (431).

Mithraism. A Persian religion, rival of Christianity. Mithra, a sun-god, mediator between God and man. Rites similar to baptism, confirmation, communion; also Sunday. For men only, but annexed cult of Magna Mater for women.

Neoplatonism. A Greek philosophy, rival of Christian theology. Ammonius Saccas, Plotinus (d. 270), Porphyry (d. 304). The vision of God attained by asceticism and meditation: mysticism. Brought into Christianity by "Dionysius the Areopagite" (about 476).

Manichæism. Another Persian religion. Dualism: life a war between good and evil. For help of man came Buddha, Zoroaster, Jesus—and Mani. Victory by asceticism. Augustine tried this religion, but abandoned it.

V

THE FATHERS FROM IGNATIUS TO AUGUSTINE

Most dates in this table before 258, and most birth-dates after that, are conjectural and approximate.

I

Ignatius,	117.
Papias,	60–135.
Polycarp,	69–155.
Justin Martyr,	100–168.
Irenæus,	130–180.

II

Clement of Alexandria,	150–215.
Tertullian,	155–222.
Origen,	185–254.
Cyprian,	200–258.

III

Eusebius of Cæsarea,	260–340.
Hilary of Poictiers,	300–367.

Athanasius,	293–373.
Basil,	330–379.
Ulfilas,	311–383.
Cyril of Jerusalem,	315–386.
Gregory of Nazianzus,	329–389.
Gregory of Nyssa,	331–396.
Ambrose,	340–397.
Martin,	316–400.
Chrysostom,	345–407.
Jerome,	340–420.
Cassian,	360–435.
Augustine,	354–430.

Printed in the United States
136706LV00003B/47/A